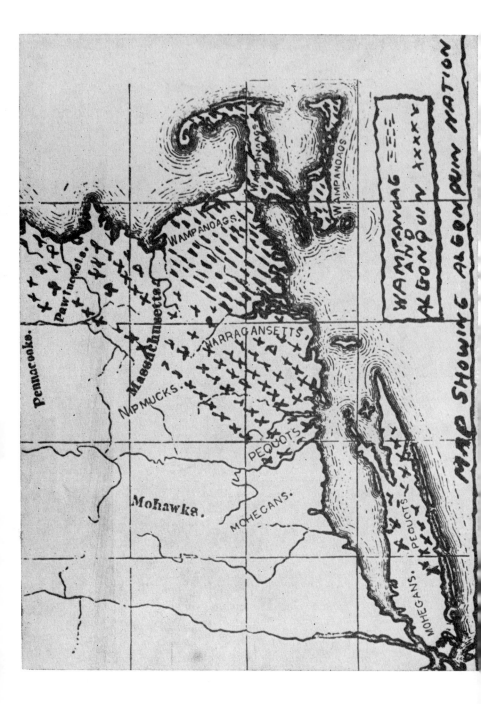

# THE WAMPANOAG
# INDIAN FEDERATION
# OF THE
# ALGONQUIN NATION

*Indian Neighbors of the Pilgrims*

# THE WAMPANOAG INDIAN FEDERATION OF THE ALGONQUIN NATION

## Indian Neighbors of the Pilgrims

By

### Milton A. Travers

DRAWINGS
BY
MARY JANE POLLOCK

*Revised Edition*

THE CHRISTOPHER PUBLISHING HOUSE
BOSTON, U.S.A.

This book is dedicated to the
Wampanoag Indian word

"KRIETTA"

An Indian word of tenderness, that
brought back in the eyes of an Indian
Maiden the memories and love of
home, the thoughts of mother, and
the wisdom of grandmother; — and
of the heritage lost  .   .   .   and,
regained!

"KRIETTA"

I heard it spoken by the lady that was
once the maiden.

# Foreword

This fascinating collection of information about the late Neolitic people who controlled and comprised the Wampanoag Indian Federation of the Algonquin Nation was compiled as a result of a deep rooted pride and loyalty to the traditions of a beloved country. It is the product of a curiosity sustained through many years of exhaustive studies, conversations and research which have resulted in a volume that has long been needed, which cried for publication, and which will become a valuable source for future seekers of knowledge about events which occurred several hundred years ago, but which played such a significant part in the germination and development of our present North American Culture.

The many early documents and sources quoted by the author in this compilation of the history of the Wampanoag Indians make interesting reading for every American and make the book the most complete record of the subject which has come to my attention.

He presents his work, *not as a scholarly and exhaustive treatise,* but as a thoroughly readable, cursive account of the impact of an advanced culture upon a primitive people.

The author, Milton A. Travers, of New Bedford, Massachusetts, presented to me, recently, about one hundred and seventy pages of typewritten manuscript, and asked me to read it and evaluate its potential merit for publication.

In connection with my hobby as an amateur archaeologist with nearly ten years of study and excavation in Bristol and Plymouth Counties, and as a student of local history, I felt competent to assure him that, in my opinion the result of his labor deserved to be recorded in print.

After several discussions, and a trial of my maiden efforts, as editor, of his material; we agreed that I would correct spelling, punctuation, inept phraseology, and similar minor matters. Responsibility for chronology, and the accuracy of sources and text, remains in his judgment.

I have greatly enjoyed this collaboration, and join the author in the hope that readers of our joint efforts may find profit and pleasure in careful or casual perusal.

On the whole, I consider it an informed and sensitive interpretation of the recent past.

HOWARD C. MANDELL,

Past President of Mass.
Archaeological Society

New Bedford, Mass.

April 11, 1957

# Chapter I

## Author's Introductory Chapter
# THE WAMPANOAG
# INDIAN FEDERATION

## Indian Neighbors of the Pilgrims

*The author at the entrance
to Anawon Rock*

*A photograph of a diorama of a typical Wampanoag Indian Village*
*Courtesy Wm. S. Fowler, Curator*
*The Bronson Indian Museum, Attleboro, Mass.*

# THE WAMPANOAG FEDERATION
## OF THE
## ALGONQUIN NATION

## INDIAN NEIGHBORS OF THE PILGRIMS

The Wampanoag Indian Tribes were a once powerful and haughty people. They and the Pequots, the
Narrangansetts, the Massachusetts, and the Pawtuck-
etts were the confederated tribes which comprised
the Algonquin Indian Nation native to New England.

The Wampanoag Federation played a great part in
the early life of the colonies, for it was they, under
the friendly leadership of the great Sachem Massasoit, who guided and helped the Pilgrims through
the perils and hardships of their first forty years on
the soil of the New World.

This present work is an attempt to compile, from
numerous scattered and nearly discarded sources,
the available historical data on this tribe. It is, of
course, *by no means complete or exhaustive;* but
relevant material from a vast body of writings and
references has been abstracted and collected in this
volume; — thus laying the foundation, perhaps, for
a fair and unprejudiced correlation and assessment
of a neglected phase of our early history.

Herein is the story of the Totem of the Wolf.

The Wampanoags owned and hunted all the lands
of the Islands of Nantucket and Martha's Vineyard,
and the mainland from Narragansett Bay and the
Providence River, from Cape Cod and the Atlantic
Ocean northerly to the Southern boundary of the

Massachusetts Tribes who lived around the bay that now bears their name. This northern boundary of the Wampanoag country seems to have included the towns of Attleboro, Rehoboth, and Swansea; and all of the counties of Nantucket, Dukes, Barnstable, Plymouth, Bristol, and a considerable part of Norfolk County in Massachusetts; together with all of Bristol and Newport Counties, and East Providence, in Rhode Island.

The Wampanoags were at first referred to as the Pokanoket Tribe, but it was later learned that the word, "Pokanoket," meant, "land of the bitter water bays and coves," and was the descriptive title applied to their whole area. The name Wampanoag is said to mean, "The Coastal or Eastern People".

Thereby, a Wampanoag Indian termed himself an Easterner from the Pokanoket country, with his residence in any one of the several tribute tribes or villages owning allegiance to the Wampanoag Sachem.

In the Pokanoket country the three principal villages which have been mentioned as among Massasoit's dwelling places, and in and about which he undoubtedly spent much of his time, were Sowams, where the town of Warren, R. I. is now; Montaup (Mt. Hope), now the town of Bristol, R. I.; and Kickimuit on the river of the same name, and within the limits of the present town of Swansea, Massachusetts.

The first visit by the Colonists to the Indian leader's village was made in July of the year 1621, when Edward Winslow and Stephen Hopkins were sent on a visit to Sowams, the seat of the Sachem, Massasoit. They brought him gifts and negotiated tentative plans for trade agreements. Massasoit mentioned that all of his thirty tribes would participate. It is clear, from his remark, that he claimed that many tribute villages under his leadership.

Three or four years before the landing of the Pilgrims, the Wampanoags and the Massachusetts Federations had suffered terrible losses of population due to a plague that swept their country. Many of the tribes were completely wiped out. In addition, within the same years, they suffered near defeat at the hands of the Narragansett Federation. In 1615, Massasoit's people and lands were cruelly attacked and raided by a group of Indians called "Tarratines" (believed to have been Penobscots).

We mention this now, because we have found that there were sufficient tribes listed in various sources to bring the total to well over the thirty mentioned in most accounts of the Wampanoag Federation.

Many variations in the spelling of Indian names and terms occur in different sources and, not infrequently, in the same source. The Wampanoag Indians had no alphabet and no written language. Contemporary English recorders were forced to render, as best they could, unfamiliar gutturals, whistling aspirates, and other vocal sounds which have no counterpart in our language.

As a simple example, the present town of Hyannis, Massachusetts and the nearby hamlet called Wianno each trace the derivation of the present place name to that of a tribal sagamore referred to in early writings as Iyanough. Still it was found in other sources as, Iyannos, Hyanos, Jannos, Yannis, Highannus and Hyanus.

As an example of greater complexity, the spelling of the name of the present town of Acushnet, Massachusetts, has been accurately transcribed from written and printed matter in church, town, and court records, and in deeds, wills, leases and letters, in no less than forty-two variations, including Accuishnent, Accusshaneck, Acoosnet, Acquechinook, Acuquoshnet, Quishnet, and Cushnet, and all meaning the same!

An article compiled by the Smithsonian Institute attributes to the Wampanoag Federation the fealty of thirty lesser tribute tribes.

The following list includes names of some of the better known tribes belonging at some time to the Wampanoag Federation, together with some of the smaller villages. (Others we will list later.) These include, Agawam, Assameekg, Assawompsett, Assonet, Acoosnet, Apponagansett, Capowack, Chappaquiddicks, Coaxet, Cohannet, Cooxissett, Cowsumpsit, Kittaumut, Coquasquscit, Mattakeeset, Mettapoiset, Miacomit, Montaup, Manamoyk, Monponset, Nemasket, Nashanekammuck, Ohkonkemme, Pachade, Pocasset, Quittaub, Sakonnett, Sancheacantacket, Seconchqut, Shawomet, Shimoah, Sowams, Talhanio, Toikiming, Wacchimuqut, Wawayontat, Nausett, Patuxet, Manomet and Sippican.

We repeat that it is our belief that many of these and still others were not mentioned in some records because, in Massasoit's time, the plague (believed to have been smallpox) had decimated many tribes. Thereby, when the great Sachem mentioned to Mr. Winslow that he had thirty tribute tribes under his leadership, he may have meant the remaining total at the time. For example, it might be pointed out here that the famous Indian ally, Squanto, was the *sole survivor* of the Patuxets, who, years before the plague, had their village in the same spot chosen by the Pilgrims as the site of Plymouth.

The place of origin and the racial derivation of the Indians encountered by the Pilgrims are still questions being studied and debated among anthropologists and archaeologists. It is generally agreed, however, that they were of Mongoloid stock, and their ancient ancestors emigrated, in glacial or post glacial times, from some part of Asia to Alaska, and thence, in the course of many millenia, southward and eastward throughout the Americas.

Be that as it may, the views of the Pilgrims, and of William Penn, and other early writers, were interesting, and are therefore included to help the reader to adjust his thinking backward in time to the 17th century.

Some believed that, from the great similarity of the manners and customs of the Indians and those of the Jews, the Indian tribes who roamed the wilderness of North America were in part descendants of the lost tribes of Judah. Their belief in this theory, according to Roger Williams, was based on the similarity of many of their manners and customs. "Their religious emblems were nearly of the same import; . . . their rites and ceremonies varied very little in essential qualities; — and, too, the languages seemed, in some instances, basically the same."

From William Penn's works in his 2nd Vol. Page 80, written in the year 1682, we get this quote, "I found them (the Indians) in great countenance with the Jewish race; and their children of so lively a resemblance to them, that a man would think himself in Duke's Place or Berry's Place in London where he seeth them."

Another early historian by the name of Adair, through personal contact and residence among the early Indians, had a great opportunity to notice the idioms of their language. He took great pains to show the similarity of the Hebrew with the Indian languages, both in their roots and general construction. He insisted that many of the Indian words were purely Hebrew.

Winslow, in a story about Massasoit, mentioned that the great chief called him "Wins—no", noting that the Indians had difficulty in pronouncing the "L's"; — and we note that Orientals, especially the Chinese, always seemed to have difficulty pronouncing words with the letter "L".

It is well established that our southern Indians believed that their old time ancestors came from beyond a great and turbulent water, and that nine out of ten of their nation passed over this body of water, but the remainder refused.

The Indians also believed that when they lived far to the west they were ruled by a king who had two sons; and that a group of their ancestors swore allegiance to one of these sons, and traveled a great distance with him for many years.

Finally they approached a great river, crossed it, and set up their villages in the new land.

Mr. McKenzie in his "History of the Fur Trade" on Page 113 had the following to say on this subject, ". . . they had a tradition among them, that they

originally came from another country, inhabited by
wicked people, and had traversed a great lake, which
was narrow, shallow, and full of Islands, where they
had suffered great hardships and much misery, it
being always winter, with ice and deep snows . . . At
a place where they called the 'Coppermine River',
they made the first land, the ground was covered with
copper, over which a body of earth had since been
collected to the depth of a man's height.   They
believed also that in ancient times their ancestors
had lived until their feet were worn out with walking, and their throats with eating.   They described
a deluge, when the waters spread over the whole
earth, except the highest mountain, on top of which
they were preserved."

There is a peninsula of Eastern Siberia that
stretches southerly into the Pacific between the
Behring Sea on the East and the sea of Okhotsk
on the West.   The peninsula is long and narrow,
swelling out toward the middle and terminating in
a point only seven miles distant from the northern-
most of the Kurile Islands.   A chain of volcanic
mountains runs down the center. The coast is formed
of rugged, precipitous cliffs.

The Kamchadales who lived there had manners
not unlike those of the North American Indians.  The
principal of these islands, including Kurile, are those
called Behrings, Copper Islands, Aleutian Islands
and Fox Island.   Copper Islands derived its name
from the great deposit of copper found there.

Modern scientific opinion endores this route as
the most probable avenue over which many species
of animals, some of which are now extinct, and the
wandering hunters who followed and lived upon

some of this game, came to America many thousands of years ago.

It is a sad thing to contemplate, in our times, the thoughtless and inconsiderate treatment of the helpless descendants of those *first American humans,* who struggle to survive on the Reservations to which we have relegated them.

# Chapter II

## THE TOTEM
## OF THE
## WOLF

*Wampanoag Indian Women Building Homes
at a New Village Site*

*Courtesy Dr. William S. Fowler
Curator, Bronson Museum,
Attleboro, Mass.*

*With his stone adze, a typical Wampanoag Indian puts finishing
touches to his dugout as his family watches.*

# THE WAMPANOAG INDIANS

It is not hard to visualize the early countryside of the Indian as it appeared to the eyes of the first white visitors. One has only to picture the whole area of the Pokanoket country as an expanse of wooded splendor with here and there a clearing or meadow around the various villages of the aborigines, and each village connected to the others by a network of footpaths.

The woods were filled with all types of game. The rivers and streams offered up limitless amounts of fish and water fowl. Flocks of upland game such as quail, partridge and wild turkeys were easily trapped and killed. Fur bearing animals roamed the woods in abundance. In all, the Indian had at his doorstep an unlimited store-house for his well being.

In a journey through the early Pokanoket country the traveler would have noticed, scattered along the inland coast and on the banks of bays and rivers many a typical Wampanoag Indian Village surrounded by clearings and cultivated fields. Arranged around the center left open for the performance of the village games and ceremonies, were the wetus constructed of saplings set firmly in the ground and bent together, fastened at the top and covered with bark or mats. Some were cone-shaped holding only a single family. Others resembled a covered arbor varying in length from twenty to one hundred feet.

The wigwams were pitched closely together and the village seldom occupied more than three to four acres. For the sake of warmth, the inside was dug a few inches lower than the outside and covered with pine needles, "cat-tail" down, skins, etc. Within the

wigwams and arranged around the walls were the woven baskets that held the corn; stone or earthen household utensils, wooden pails, and the low-raised bunks lined with soft boughs and skins.

In the center of the interior blazed the fire which served for cooking and for warmth. It was kept constantly burning and the smoke was allowed to find its natural outlet through a hole in the roof.

The domestic life of the inhabitants of such a dwelling amidst the dust, dirt and fleas, and constant banter of the children, the free running dogs, and the sooty smoke from both pipe and fire that unquestionably filled the interior, was far from our idea of comfortable living. But, the Wampanoag Indian spent most of his time in the clean outdoors in the healthful pursuits of his livelihood and this indeed tended to balance and compensate the unhealthful qualities brought on in respect to their living quarters.

The Wampanoag Indians were all customarily dressed in moccasins and small breeches of tanned deerskin fringed and embroidered with wampum. Excepting for the women who wore shirts, the body was left bare above the waist and was always heavily greased. The Sachems, or chiefs as we call them, were distinguished from the ordinary members during tribal ceremonial gatherings and events in that their dress consisted of heavy belts and straps of wampum that were the symbols of their office. The Wampanoag leaders never wore the long headdress so typical of the western aborigine.

In the winter, mantles of fox, beaver, deer and raccoon, with the fur side turned inward close to the body, were worn by the Indians. Their hair was

arranged in a variety of fashions according to the particular fancy of the individual. Some shaved on one side of the head allowing the hair to grow along the other side. Some left only a ridge in the middle, extending from the forehead to the neck, and kept short and straight with various paints and bear grease resembling the appearance of the Roman Helmet. Other men of the tribe shaved all their head, leaving only a small tuft of the scalp lock on the back of the scalp.

Their food was basically that of the flesh of fish and wild fowl and game, corn, beans, peas, squash, ground nuts, berries and acorns.

The squaws prepared these foods in a variety of ways without regard to the appearance of the serving. The bones and entrails of the fish and smaller animals were seldom removed before cooking. Two of their common dishes were later adopted by the white man and are used to this very day. One is corn or samp which consisted of corn meal and currants boiled with water to a paste and served plain or fried. The other dish was succotash made of boiled corn, beans and fat to which fish was sometimes added. To their corncakes they usually added whatever fruits were in season. The addition of wild strawberries smashed and ground into the meal was always a tasty favorite. They ate their corn in various stages of its growth, tender ripe to the dried kernel.

Shellfish, crabs and lobsters were usually prepared over the hot stones and sea weed; and the method of preparing the basic shellfish and foods of today's clambakes over these steaming hot stones is another custom handed down by the Wampanoag Indian.

The favorite dish of the Indians was a stew made
of all kinds of flesh from birds, animals and fish and
vegetables boiled in the same pot and to which was
added for thickening, the meal of powdered acorns,
walnuts, etc., that were easily gathered in the woods
nearby.

Fire was used instead of bedclothes during the
night, and the first member of a household to awake,
usually assumed the task of rekindling the fire.
When they had bad dreams it was believed that
one of their gods was threatening them, and should
one be awakened by such a dream they immediately
all fell to prayer and lamentations to be preserved
from the wrath of the particular god whom they
believed might be angry with them at that moment.

The door of the abode was open day or night.
Instead of shelves, they had several baskets wherein
they put all their household things.  On the walls
were hung big bags or sacks made of grass, roots,
or willow branches which had capacities from five
to six bushels.

A Community steam bath was a customary ritual.
It was built in the side of a hill, close by to a pool
or river.  They would first heat the stones within
and then go in, sometimes as many as twenty at a
time, wherein they would remain until a sufficient
sweat was brought up, whereupon they would run
out and dive into the cold water.  They did this to
sweat and clean their skins and purge their bodies
of all impurities both physical and spiritual; but,
generally, in personal sanitation they were usually a
bit slack.  During one visit of the Indians to the
Pilgrims, one gentleman wrote and said that he had
seen a great half-naked Indian sitting within a small

group picking lice from his body and biting them dead between his teeth.

Much as is the custom today among women, the Indian maiden painted her face with all sorts of color that she believed a help to her better appearance.  They used the pine bark and red earth for this purpose.  Also the juices of wild berries mixed with various powders produced the desired effects.

The Squaws did all the work.  The men devoted all their time to hunting and provided for the general safety of the family.

With the help of pebbles or grains of corn the native could reckon into great numbers.  They were very affectionate to their children.  During rare moments of leisure, the women amused themselves by weaving of mats with which they decorated the interior of the wigwam, or by making soapstone pots, kettles and baskets.

Each village had its own priests or medicine men — "Pow-Wow" was their name for them — and for their services they were paid in wampum or commodities of the hunt or labor.  These men at times effected what seemed to be miraculous cures.  One of the systems used was to howl and roll and perform different gymnastics together with chants and dances; and in some cases of high fever, dunking in the cold water revived or cured the patient one way or another.

These Pow-Wows were fakirs of real ability and were important members of each village, advisors in all dealings.  They were the lawyers and chaplains of their times, as well as the doctors.

Nearly all the natives were addicted to smoking and carried their pipes and tobacco with them at all times. Their pipes were anywhere from a few inches to two feet long and sometimes were carved with figures or men and beasts. Taking care of the crop of tobacco was the extent of the men's agricultural enterprise. The women and children worked the rest of the crop.

In planting their corn they would place a dead herring in each hill as fertilizer and they would be sure to plant the seed deep enough to prevent birds from eating it up; and as an added precaution watch-houses were always set up in the center of the field and it fell to the young boys and girls to stay within them and frighten the marauders off. As we said, the women set and planted, weeded and generally tendered the growing and harvesting of the crop.

Their implements were of the crudest and they labored hard and long with hoes made of clam and quahog shells and stone fastened to a length of branch. They were expert gardeners, considering what they had to work with. Each family planted and tended its own plot, which in some cases were three or four acres; and it is said the gardens were weeded and neat.

Whenever land was cleared many people got together to plow and it is said that some stone walls built by Indian labor still stand to this very day.

The aborigine was very observant of the moon and stars. If the season was dry they would sometimes fall into prayer for as long as ten days at a time beseeching their gods for rain.

They would point to the sun for the time of day. They would divide the year into spring, summer, autumn, (or the falling of the leaf) and winter. They would number the years by any of these four periods, for they had no name for the year; subdividing these, they would count the year by lunar months, or moons. Their name for the sun and the moon were one and the same, with addition of day and night, (as the day sun, or moon, the night sun). They reckoned the day by three sensible differences of the sun; — as the sun coming out — mid-day, and sun is dead, or sunset. Midnight was half way between the sun going in and coming out of the water.

They began their ecclesiastical year at the first appearance of the first new moon or the vernal equinox. The Wampanoags paid great regard to the first appearance of every new moon. They stipulated the various seasons of the year from the planting and ripening of the fruits and nuts. The green-eared moon was the most beloved or sacred, and when the first fruits became sanctified, by being annually offered up; and from this period they counted their beloved or spiritual things.

They were a happy and gregarious people who believed that the brain was the seat of the soul for the temper of the brain in quick apprehensions and acute judgments was a gift of the most high and sovereign god and creator.

Indeed the sun was their adored god of great divinity and power. They loved the god of the southwest winds because he brought them the warmest of their climate. They believed that his wind came directly from the dwelling place of their gods which they earnestly believed would be the happy hunting grounds of their own souls after death.

They moved their villages at various seasons or when flies plagued them or whenever the chieftain of the village died.

It has been noted that the pain of toothache was believed to be the only thing that could make an Indian cry.

The persons who could tell them news of events past and present in their own tongue were called "Minatou" (wise ones). At story sessions which usually occurred in the evenings around the fire nearly every day, the story teller was the most admired person of all.

In the Fall during the great Autumnal Pow-Wow, all the natives of the village would sit around the speaker in a large circle smoking their pipes contentedly and never would they think of interrupting for a moment.

An Indian customarily carried with him a basket of corn and flint stones to make a fire, a hatchet to cut down a tree, to make a shelter or shed for comfort while he hewed himself a dugout, etc. From the basket that he carried he would bring his meal of corn, and his tobacco; then resume his business of the day that was wrought and aided by the contents of that basket.

The Wampanoags were great swimmers and were nearly as much at home in the water as they were on land.

Their fishing nets were made of strong pliable willow whips, and they could also catch fish by shooting at them with bow and an arrow to which a long piece of root-cord was attached. Clams, oysters, crabs, lobsters and other shellfish were a great delicacy and it was not uncommon to see groups of

Indians along the shores at low water digging and
fishing for the morsels. They ate them raw, fresh
from the sand or water. Sometimes they boiled them
and mixed the broth with their bread. This, incidentally, was their only source of salt as the early
Wampanoag added no seasoning to his food.

They took great pains in their fishing, especially
in watching the tides by day or by night, and frequently they would lay their naked bodies on the
sands of the damp shore and often in the night they
woke to search their nets in the cold water. Eels
were caught in abundance by treading the mud of
the salt marshes with their naked feet and grabbing
at the fish as it squirmed underfoot.

It was customary at these times of the fishing season to go naked or wear small breeches or coverlets.
The women wore aprons about their waists and so
did the men at times. Children as a rule wore no
clothing until they reached the age of twelve.

Indoors they would leave off the best skins. Their
head gear consisted of ornaments of turkey feathers
and beads made usually by the old men of the tribe.
Shoes and stockings were made of deerskin which
were well oiled so as to keep out the snow and
water. They tanned their own leather and painted
their deerskins for summer wear.

They believed that their gods were the authors
of all things and if they should lose a child, or should
any other misfortune befall them, it was felt that
the god was angry with them. Their gods were
many and varied. Among their deities not mentioned
before, was the sun god, the moon god, the sea god,
the fire god, etc. They felt that the spark which
gave fire was in itself a bit of the divine god of
fire.

An Indian ate only when he felt hungry; but they staged at times great feasts to celebrate various events and gods. These gatherings were gay but somewhat frenzied affairs as they were always accompanied by the rhythmic dance and applause so peculiar to natives of the forest. At feasts or gatherings many speeches were made. The Indian leaders were noted for their eloquence and descriptive talks. All speeches were usually very solemn. Their priests and old men nearly always spoke of peace, war and the various gods.

The Wampanoag Sachemship constituted a true monarchy and succession was by birthright alone since time immemorial. There were two other levels of lesser society: — the warrior leaders (panseis) or sagamores that included chiefs of the tribute tribes holding special rights and privileges; and the ordinary people (sannops) who had no rights at all. This system was unique and peculiar to the tribes of the Algonquin Nation. Most of the other tribes in North America had a political structure that was more democratic.

The Sachem of the Wampanoag Federation was indeed an absolute monarch, but he would decide no great issue without first consulting the lesser tribal chiefs and sagamores in his federation. No matter, his law was carried out in lieu of punishment by whipping, or death by beheading.

In domestic life the Wampanoag practiced polygamy to an extent, but many did not observe it as their prerogative even though such was generally accepted. The male Indian could leave one and take another woman when he so desired. Adultery was considered the cardinal vice, whereupon the husband had the right to flog his wife in the public square as complete punishment for the crime. Wives at times left husbands for mere displeasure and could leave one and take another for no major reason.

It was believed that the Indian practiced polygamy because it was a show of wealth and an expedient in getting his work done, and as Roger Williams put it; "due to their long sequestering themselves from their wives after conception, until the child be weaned, which with some is long after a year old."

The courtship was natural and upon the choice being made, the male first paid his respects and intention to the parents by making gifts of food and skins. A necklace of wampum proffered by the Indian and accepted by the maiden sanctified the marriage which could be for trial, or permanent. The nuptials had next to be given the blessings of the Chief, and the ceremony was complete. The bride's family always offered up a dowry. If they were poor, relations or others were expected to contribute toward it.

Their money was of two kinds; — one was white, made of the stem or stock of the quahog which was rounded and rubbed on stones after the outer shell had been broken off. Six of these beads of white wampum were later bartered to the worth of an English penny. They bored holes in them and strung them like necklaces. When strung in this fashion they were called wampumpeag (actually plural for wampum).

Black money was made of the shellfish called, "henfish", but better known to us as quahog. They used only the black pearly bit of this shell. Three of these black beads made, in exchange, an English penny. The wampumpeag was usually worn as ornaments on the head, arms, waists, and around the neck.

Each member of the tribe had his duty to perform. Some of the men would make the implements of war. Others would attend to the hunting and fishing, but it was usually left to the older males to gather and store the shells which would be later made into wampum by the women.

While on the warpath or engaged in tours of hunting or fishing, parched corn and maple sugar were usually carried. This food moistened with water from a spring or pond, together with what game they killed along the way, helped them subsist for long periods of time while absent from the village. This was food for the journey, later converted by the English into Johnny Cake.

In anticipation of the long cold winters, the Wampanoag Indian provided stores of parched corn, maize, nuts and dried meats of fish and game which they stored in pits dug into the sides of hills. These were the so-called root cellars of the Indians that were scattered in various places close by their dwelling areas. These cellars were built by the squaws and their locations were usually kept from the men.

Whenever death occurred to the head of a family or his squaw the normal home life of that family was immediately curtailed. They broke up their wigwam and moved in with relations or friends and remained with them during a mourning period. Even though these natives held to a belief that the soul lived forever after them, they would never give the name of a deceased person to any other member

of the tribe. The memory of the dead was sacred
to them but they rarely ever discussed the departed.
The mere profaning of a dead Sachem was motiva-
tion for inter-tribal war.

When death struck they would blacken their faces
with soot and for weeks or months, and sometimes
for a whole year they would go about with blackened
faces as a mark of mourning and sorrow. The name
of the dead was never again mentioned in public.
It was customary to wrap the corpse in mats and
place it near a shallow grave; have general lamentations where survivors cried and screamed, clasped
their hands over their mouths and laid prostrate on
the ground.

The body would then be placed within the grave
with the hands clasped over the knees. Warriors or
chiefs were usually buried in a sitting position. A
mat would then be placed near the body and on it
were placed the possessions considered most useful
to the departed soul. His skin coat would then be
hung close by and left there to rot, in the belief that
the soul would need the cloak for warmth in its
journey to the other world. To them, evidence of
its departure was surely proved by the crumbling
and rotting away of the clothing as the spirit was
clutching to clothe itself.

Another burial ceremony was practiced by these
natives. Each tribe had its own method of disposing
of the body according to the beliefs and supersti-
tions handed down. We are not certain that the
whole of the following method was carried out by
the Wampanoag tribes, but we do have evidence of
cremation as a result of findings uncovered at the
site of Assawompsett Pond by field workers of the
Massachusetts Archaeological Society.

First, the Indians dug a shallow grave and over this grave they built a tall platform of pine trees constructed somewhat like a shack with four upright walls and a flat roof. On the roof they placed the body and left it there exposed to the elements, the birds of prey, etc., to assist in the natural process of decay, leaving nothing but the bones. At some later day when the relations of the deceased felt the body had been exposed long enough, they returned and piled upon this platform along side the skeleton all the possessions of the dead one, his furs, weapons, tools, baskets, pots and hunting implements. At this point it was the duty of the medicine man, (Pow-Wow) to perform a very solemn ceremony climaxed by setting the structure afire. The flames would rapidly burn and rise up through the entire structure consuming as much as possible until the bier collapsed into the grave below. The assembled Indians would then very religiously scrape up all the ashes into the grave, cover it with turf; offer further lamentations and leave never to mention the name of the dead one publicly again.

As a race, the Indians were very simple and mild mannered. They were tall, slight and agile and their eyes were jet black and so was the hair that ordinarily hung straight. Their skin was copper colored, with faces giving off an expression sometimes gloomy, and sometimes noble. Armed with bows and arrows they knew all the habits of the birds and beasts and they ran and walked through the woods just as stealthily as any of God's creatures.

The Indian squaw was a very devoted wife and mother who really adored her family. Hers was a handsome face with eyes very small and far apart. The forehead was low under coarse black hair. Her

mouth was large and readily broke into a pleasing
smile. The skin was coppertone. Wherever the
mother went she would carry her baby with her
in a cradle that was either strapped around her
back or hung nearby as she worked. The cradle
was made of thin wood and she fastened the baby,
(papoose) in it with a ribbon of linden tree bark.
She lined the cradle with sweet smelling grass from
the meadows and decorated it gayly with colored
porcupine quills and shells, beads and rattles.

One of the early writers and observers of the Wampanoags, a man by the name of Brereton, described
the squaws as such in one of his works: "Their
women such as we saw, which were but three in all,
built low of stature, their eyebrows, hair, apparel,
and manner of wearing like the men; fat, and very
well favored, and much did delight our company."

Mr. John Joselyn in another early account wrote,
"The men are somewhat horse-faced, and generally
faucious without beards, but the women of them,
many of them have very good features seldom without 'come to me' in their countenance. All of them
black-eyed and short teeth and very white; their hair
was black, thick and long, broad breasted; handsome, straight bodies, and slender, considering their
constant loose habits; their limbs cleanly, straight
and of convenient stature, — generally as plump as
partridges; and saving here and there one of modest
deportment."

William Wood had this to say about the women:
"To satisfy the curious eye of the women readers,
who otherwise might think their sex forgotten, — they
(the men) do not admit them as their equals, though
their qualities and industrious deservings may justly

claim that their eminence, and command better usage and more conjugal esteem; (sic) their person and feature being every way correspondent, their qualifications were more excellent, being more loving, pitiful, and modest, mild, provident, and laborious than their lazy husbands."

This description written by a sailor on one of Gosnold's early trips gives a generalization of the Wampanoag Indian brave: "These people as they are exceedingly courteous, gentle of disposition, and well conditioned, excel all others that we have seen; so for shape of body and lovely favor, they excel all the other people of America. Of stature much higher than we; a complexion or color much like dark olive. Their eyebrows and hair black, which they wear long tied up behind in a knot whereupon they prick feathers of fowl, in fashion of a crownette; some of them are black thin bearded. They make beards of the hair of beasts; and one of them offered a beard of their making for that of one of our sailors, for his that grew on his face, which because it was of red color they judged to be none of their own. They are quick eyed, and steadfast in their looks, fearless of others harms, as intending none themselves; some of the meanest sort given to filching which the very name of savages (not weighing their ignorance in good nor ill) may be easily excused. They wear garments of deerskin close around and close to their necks."

The Indian squaw was not as good a housekeeper as one can easily imagine under the circumstances within which she lived. Her cooking utensils were never washed. After each meal they were merely scraped and set aside for the next meal. If she was the wife of a Sachem, the most treasured object in her wigwam was the little bundle of dried skins that hung high up on the walls away from the reach of the children. This was indeed a very precious part of the whole tribe's way of life!

Sometimes in the early morning just before setting out on a hunting trip, or before any major event, this brown bundle of skins drew the attention of all. At times the great Sachem would stand in front of this sacred bundle and raise both arms and call out to it in prayer beseeching consultation. At other times it was taken and hung in the square and the Pow Wow (medicine man) in all his paints and wampum danced before it and sang and shouted imploringly to it. Later this same priest would pause and in a loud voice proclaim to all that the bundle of skins was indeed a god, (Manitto). If the sacred bundle had offered to him a revelation, he would then disclose it to the waiting assembly.

In the warrior's wigwam the main object of admiration was the number of enemy scalps in his collection. These were the trophies of his ability on the war path. . . . The more he had the greater warrior he was believed to be.

A great Sachem of an Indian Federation such as the Wampanoags was an absolute monarch and his orders were obeyed explicitly; but we do know that he never made any decision that involved his people until he first got the opinion and consent of the subordinate chiefs and the various Sagamores or Panseis. The Warriors of the Wampanoag Federation seems to have included the following rank; at the head, of course, was the Great Sachem. He had as his "general" or "captain" a leading Panseis, or Missinnege (i.e. Anawon). The group of subordinate

Panseis included the Sagamores of the tribes. Sagamores were those tribute chiefs who held sway over
two or more sub-tribes of the Federation, (i. e. Corbitant, Tuspaquin, Aspinet, Epanow and Iyanough).
Nevertheless, it appears that a leader of any of the
tribute tribes was sometimes called a Sachem. Hobbamock, by virtue of his being a special "envoy" in
attendance to the Colonists, held the rank of either
Sagamore or Panseis.

At any time a war was contemplated or about to
break out among the Indians, the great Sachem himself would cover his body with blackening and walk
out naked into the woods to pray and fast alone for
several days. When he returned pale and thin from
fasting, he would recount in full the stories of his
dreams and the great deeds performed within these
dreams. If his dreams happened to contain the participation of a powerful bird of prey or animal, this
was taken by all as a sure sign of victory. He would
then send out his messengers carrying bundles of
arrows dipped in blood which was the signal for all
to hasten to his seat for a council of war. This meeting or court, they called, Miawene.

The Panseis and their followers lost no time in
obeying the summons. In the Wampanoag Federation there were at least forty tribes under the one
great Sachem and they would come along with as
many warriors as they could safely muster without
leaving their own particular village in jeopardy.
The Sachem would prepare a great feast for them.
This feast was called the Nickommo. It invariably
preceded the Miawene.

It is not hard to imagine that sight. Masters of all
they could survey within miles, they rested before a
campfire with little boys passing them bits of food

and delicacies. Some of the warriors wore feathers of brightest hues. For leggings they had deerskins fringed at the side and a jacket of doeskin gaily embroidered with beads of wampum. Others wore skins tied around the waist like aprons with a pocket in front and one in back. The hair of some was tied in long knots behind them. Many warriors had their heads shaved bare excepting for a long scalp lock. The faces of all were painted in every imaginable fashion. One might have white eyebrows with red lips and pink cheeks. Another a blue forehead with orange lips, or green lips with a yellow chin. Others had straight streaks of black and white paint up and down their faces. All glistened with bear's grease and walnut oil. This was smeared over all exposed parts of their body as a preventative to insect bites and infection.

All wore ornaments of bone with strings of wampum and enemy scalps hung from their waist. Their implements of war consisted of bows and stout arrows tipped with flint and other stone, tomahawks, spears, and war clubs embellished with sharp claws of animals and birds.

There would they sit and feast in the sunset by the light of the fire and not a word would they speak about the pending war until the great Sachem was ready to talk of it. He ate nothing all the while his men were feasting and kept off to one side smoking his pipe in silence. When the feast was ended and all the pipes lighted and he saw that all the warriors were seemingly waiting for him; then, and only then, would the Sachem rise to his feet. He now wore his ceremonial robe of doeskin heavily trimmed with beads of wampum. The thick, long royal belt of his office hung from his shoulder and at his girdle of wampum, hung all the scalps he had taken in battle.

He would begin his discourse by telling them of all the insults and hurts heaped upon his tribes by their enemy which might be any that bordered their nation. He then would plead for vengeance. He recounted his favorable dreams that promised victory if his people would take arms and follow him.

After his eloquent speech, there would be loud applause and shouts of acquiescence.

Before we go any further, we must bring to mind at this point the order in which the tribes seated themselves around this council. First the oldest of the people, the men and women together, made the first row of the semi-circle. Behind them all the lusty fighting men stood, with all the lesser Indians of the tribe surrounding them on the outside of the semi-ring. When the great Sachem had finished his appeal, next to step into the ring would be the recognized great warrior or Missinnege, captain of the Panseis, (pahnseyheys). He would jump into the ring with all the frenzy and fury that he was capable of displaying. With a spear in one hand and a tomahawk in the other, he would dance around the fire pretending to fight with the flames uttering damnations to all the several nations and tribes in the country who were their enemies at that time. At the naming of each particular enemy he would draw out a firebrand and scowl and beat over it.

In his concluding action he would flourish a bow and thank the god of the fire who was going to help him to consume that enemy. He would then leap into the air and come down, and with a mighty thrust, plummet his spear into the ring, and leave. Another warrior would leap in, go through the same gyrations but with greater effort than the first. When this warrior was finished, in jumped another, and so on and on it went until all the warriors had so manifested or vented their fury, and consented to the Sachem's leadership. They were now all sworn and engaged to fight the enemy. The great Sachem now had their word and could depend on them at any time to follow him in battle and to engage the enemy. There it was in pantomime; the frenzy, the muster, the march, the ambush, the slaughter, the scalping, the reception at home by the squaws and the old men, and the torture of the prisoners.

These sessions would always end up with a tremendous ovation. If it was decided to immediately prepare for war they would first wait for the breaking of dawn when the Pow-Wow would place the head of a wolf over his shoulders and would march out into the woods alone. (The wolf being their totem, or emblem.) He would carry with him the sacred bundle of dried skins mentioned in previous paragraphs. He would scout the forest trails cautiously. He would listen to all the sounds of the morning, and each call of the bird registered an important notice to him. If there was no cawing of the crow to be heard it was counted a good sign. Pausing, he would examine the ground on either side of him and if he saw a frog leap from the marsh or a squirrel scamper through the thicket, but saw no rattlesnakes cross his pathway, he would be pleased and feel it was also a favorable sign. A rattlesnake to the Wampanoags meant danger. If he saw all the signs adding up favorably he would return to the village. Now he would order the warriors to remove all their ornaments and with the blessings of the good signs he witnessed, he then would order the warriors with their chief at the head to proceed single file to seek out and fight their enemies.

While on the warpath they carried neither baggage nor provisions other than the ground corn meal and maple sugar which they mixed with water from a spring forming a doughy paste and called by them "bread for the journey". Their weapons as we said were the same implements used for the hunt and consisted basically of a crude spear, tomahawk, wooden club, and, of course, the bow and arrow.

The warrior was prepared for battle from his earliest childhood, and no greater honor could come to him than by performing great and brave deeds in battle. The Wampanoag Indians summed up the duties of the ordinary brave as to always be under command and explicitly obey all orders of his leaders. He had to learn to march single-file through the forest in scattered order so as to be prepared to surround the enemy or to prevent his army from being surrounded. The warrior was indeed a good marksman and had to use expertly all the warring tools he had. He had to be a tireless runner and be prepared to endure extreme hardship and hunger without complaint. The exacting truth was required from him at all times with no exaggeration and especially so when out spying on the enemy's movements. The Indians felt it foolhardy to place a man in office who had never tried his skill and courage in actual combat. All leaders were promoted according to ability. It was a prime requisite that no person could have the absolute command of their warriors, and that the war council of their leaders should determine when and how the strategy and actual attack should be made. It, indeed, was the duty of their Panseis to lay all the plans and take advantage of the enemy in all ways. It was also the duty of these captains to prepare and deliver speeches to the men in order to inspire and encourage them. Each officer was trained to see that there was very little time left to the enemy to gather his forces together after setbacks. But in doing so they must at all times endeavor to save their own men; and therefore, should never bring on an attack without considerable advantage, or without what appeared to them to insure victory, and that, with a loss of as few warriors as possible. If at any time these leaders should have been proved wrong in their judgment and found themselves to lose a great many braves in any one encounter, it would be their duty to retreat and wait for greater opportunity of victory.

No matter what the outcome of the battle, whether victory or defeat, when they returned home, their people were anxiously waiting for them. Prisoners suffered as much humiliation as was possible. They were forced to run the gauntlet of screaming old men, women and children who formed a corridor through which the captured were forced to run while the victor's families clubbed and tormented them mercilessly. Stories of the battle remained for many days and years as prime entertainment for the whole tribe, and the scalps taken from their unfortunate victims were coveted as trophies of the battle.

One of the best loved seasons of the Wampanoag Indians was that of Autumn when the great Sachem of the tribes always ordered one of the most important feasts or councils of the year, called by the Wampanoags, Nikommosachmiawene. (The feast and court ordered by the Sachem.) The inevitable council fire was ordered and the warriors and their families would sit about it in a ring composed in the same order and fashion as the War Council. It was during this meeting that the history of the tribes was recounted with recent activities appended.

The oldest male child of each warrior was cere-
moniously seated along with his father so that he
missed nothing of the history of the tribe as read
by the chiefs from their royal wampum belt.

It was the custom to have the histories of their
tribes depicted on the broad bands of wampum
belts worn by the Sachem or other tribute chiefs.
It was passed around the group from one leader to
another and read aloud, each interpreting the events
depicted on it. The notes on the belts were in the
forms of pictures and designs worked in colored
beads which told of all the "Totems" or happenings
during the time of their ancestors to the present.

Totems in principle were the Indian's coat of
arms, showing various devices, just as the nations
of today. For example; Russia has the Bear, England the Lion, the United States the Eagle, etc. . . .
Thereby, it was much the same with the Indians.
One tribe would choose as a badge the beaver,
another the fox, the hare, deer or the moose. Because
the Wampanoags chose the Wolf, they were known
as "The Totem of the Wolf."

These royalties (the wampum belts) depicted in
designs of wampum the great victories, and the
mighty warriors who gained glory on the warpath
before them. They told, also, of the defeats and loss
of territory, etc. They told of the days of famine, sickness and plague . . . in short, these were the only
historical documents of their lives and that of their
ancestors before them. This was their precious
heritage for the descendants to keep and pass on
and on to posterity. It was the sacred duty of the
great Sachem to guard and preserve these royalties.

Indeed, this was the only record kept by the Wampanoag Indians. Here for the reader, is the key to why there is no complete record as to how the Indians of this locality lived the many years before the Colonists came to New England. Unfortunately, no white man ever learned to read the esoteric outlines of the royal belts of the Wampanoags.

In a later chapter dealing with Anawon, Missinnege of the Federation, we will describe in more detail these Wampanoag Royalties and their ultimate disposition.

The early Wampanoags lived an idyllic life here in the forests and bays of Massachusetts including Cape Cod, which they termed the "land and waters of the storms". In a sense they pursued a way of life that most people of today would like. Despite infrequent inter-tribal war, they had very few cares or worries. They spent their days as leisurely as possible. They ate only when they were hungry, as they had no set periods for meals. They had no domestic fowl, and the dog was their only domesticated animal. They loved eels because they were juicy and sweet. Whenever they felt hungry or craved a certain meal of flesh they simply went out into the woods surrounding their village and hunted for it. The bow and arrow was their major implement of the hunt. No matter what the journey they always carried with them a basket containing smaller tools, such as knives, etc., that always would come in handy if they had a mind to camp away from their wigwams.

The making of a canoe was always a big event in their way of life but it was a fairly easy object to make. They first cut down a small pine sapling and fashioned a long frame of it bending and tying the points together with the roots of spruce trees. Then they stripped the bark of the white birch tree that grew in abundance close by the fresh water ponds. With the finer strands of tree roots and hemp and with the aid of sharp bone-needles, they sewed the bark to the framework. From the pine trees they gathered up the balsam pitch and smeared it into the overlapping cracks and seams of the bark covering. For decoration, they merely searched out the lair of the small hedgehog or porcupine and used its dyed quills of red, white, orange, with colors obtained from the ochre of the earth or juice of berries. They then sewed the quills on to the canoe in various designs that met their fancy at the moment.

Their fishing in fresh water ponds was done mostly by night and by the light of a torch which was carried by one of the occupants of the canoe or dugout. Upon spying a pickerel or pike the fisherman lost no time upon dispatching a spear into the fish, and with the aid of an attached line he hauled in the catch. Groups of canoeists would drive in larger fish like bass that frequently came into the salt marshes and head it toward narrow inlets where they had set up traps made from the willow tree. Once the fish were caught in the trap, the Indians would jump in bodily and gaff it to shore with the aid of bone grapples.

In hunting they were proficient in setting traps for the fur bearing animals like the weasel, beaver, mink, fox, rabbit, raccoon, etc. Deer was a prized game which they hunted with bow and arrow. Being mimics of exceptional quality, the Indians could coax much of their game toward them by imitating their various calls. Because they valued the feathers of the wild turkey and had much use for them as ornaments, and for fear that they might mutilate them otherwise, they caught them in traps by luring them to a spot where they had sprinkled corn. To catch the smaller birds a length of hemp or root attached to a small stone was used, where they swung it with deadly aim at the bird of their choice. Many of the large and cumbersome animals like the moose, were easily caught during periods of heavy snow. The hunters would chase and frighten the animal, finally exhaust it, and then club it dead.

The biggest hunt of the season was always conducted in the fall just before the Autumn Council. During this hunt many Indians would band together and go out to get the stores for the winter months that lay ahead. These groups had systematic ways of hunting and trapping the various animals as mentioned above. This big hunt was done in stages. One day would be for the killing of animals, the next for fowl, and the next for fishing, etc.

In the summer the villages would be moved to the shores of ponds, rivers and bays. In the fall before the big hunt they were already moving inland to the warmth of the forest and it was here in these villages that the game was brought for the squaws to quarter and prepare. After the days of the great hunt were over, it then was time for the Sachem to proclaim the Autumn Council (Nikommosachmiawene).

They loved the fall season. What food there was that could not be stored for the winter was immediately put to use for the great feast of all the tribes. While the squaws were preparing this banquet the children ran merrily around the fields or listened to stories of the hunts as told by their brave fathers. Some of the men would retire into the amusement of their many games. This period of happy leisure following the hunt and just before the great feast, was called by the squaws, Hawkswawney.

After all the speeches were made and the history read for posterity's sake, the merriment would commence. It was much like a fair of these days. They had wrestling matches, football games, games of quoits, foot races, target shooting for the young brave, games of bowl and counters, and games of plumb stones. The medicine man would bewitch them by swallowing fire and sharp arrows. He would, to the wonder of all assembled, mesmerize some child and as quickly bring him back to the living. These Pow-Wows were very clever men and depended a great deal on the payment of wampum for their mystifying feats, and skills at curing the ill. At these autumn gatherings they had many strange and happy dances depicting imaginary gods and events. Boys provided the notes of music from their flutes and whistles of reeds, and the rhythmic clatter of turtle shells and other objects aided in the beat. Some of the dances were solemn and steady but most worked themselves into the gyrations and frenzied gymnastics so peculiar to their race. A popular amusement at these meetings were the tales told by the story tellers. They listened enraptured to the eloquence of their best orators; and he that told the best stories always found an admirable spot in his friend's eyes, and of course, was one of the most popular men of the tribes.

William Wood in his "New England Prospect" has handed down an interesting and long account of these games and pastimes that occupied the Indians during these feasts. While at home in their own respective villages, they took their sporting very seriously.

Mr. Wood in his description of the Indian Football games tells "Their Goales be a mile long placed on the sands, which are as even as a board; their ball is no bigger than a hand-ball, which sometimes they mount in the Aire with their naked feete, sometimes it is swayed by the multitude; sometimes also it is two days before they get a Goale, then they marke the ground they winne, and beginne there the next day. Before they come to this sport, they paint themselves, even as when they goe to warre, in pollicie to prevent future mischiefe, because no man should know him that moved his patience or accidentally hurt his person, taking away the occasion of studying revenge. Before they begin their armes be disordered, and hung upon some neighborring tree, after which they make a long scrowle on the sand, over which they shake loving hands, and with laughing hearts scuffle for victorie. While the men play the boys pipe, and the women dance and sing trophies of their husbands conquests; all being done, a feast summons their departure. It is most delight to see them play, in smaller companies, when men may view their swift footmanship, their curious tossings of the Ball, their flouncing into the water, their lubberlike wrestling, having no cunning at all in that kind, one English being able to beate ten Indians at football."

Platter or dice was the second most popular game. This sport was played at times for large stakes, — possessions, service of servitude and sometimes whole villages changed hands as a result of this gambling. Roger Williams best describes the game as follows: "They have a kind of dice which are Plumb stones painted, which they cast in a Tray with a mighty noyse and sweating. Their publique games, are solemnized with the meeting of hundreds; sometimes thousands, and consists of many varieties, none of which I durst ever be present at that I might not conntenance and partake of their folly after I once saw the evill of them. The chiefe Gamesters amongst them much desire to make their Gods side with them. . . . Therefore I have seen them keepe as a precious stone a piece of Thunderbolt, which is like unto a Chrystall, which they dig out of the ground under some Tree, Thunder Smitten, and from this stone they have an opinion of successe, and I have not heard any of these prove loosers, which I conceive may be Satan's policie, and God's holy Justice to harden them for their not rising higher from the Thunder-bolt, to the God that sends or shoots it."

Mr. Roger William's description of their gambling place reads as follows; "This Arbour or Play house is made of long poles set in the Earth, four square, sixteen or twentie foot high, on which they hang great store of their stringed money, have great staking towne against towne, and two chosen out of the rest by course to play the Game at this kind of Dice, in the midst of all their abettors, with great shouting and soleminity."

The other outdoor sport the Indians played was called "Hub Hub" which resemble dice. "Hub Hub," describes Mr. Wood, "consists of five small bones in a smooth Tray which they place on the ground before them, against which violently thumping the platter, the bones mount, changing colours with the windy whisking of their hands too and fro; which action in that sport they much use, smiting themselves on the Breast, and thighs crying Hub, Hub, Hub; they may be heard playing at this Game a quarter of a mile off."

Another popular game was a game played with straws of reeds or rushes called sometimes the Indian's game of cards in which, being able to calculate by memory, and split second observance, together with an acute ability to add rapidly, multiply and subtract, were prime requisites for success.

They were known to play a game very much like our present game of basketball where the ball was tossed into the air and over goals. Tug of war was also a great delight to them.

All phases of character considered, the Wampanoags strike one as being a happy lot with a definite culture, and very unlike the savages that generations of the unknowing have been led to believe. When one thinks of these Indians as savages one no doubt dwells in thoughts of the terrible atrocities performed during battles, but one is apt to forget that they at first were indeed friendly to all white men. In fact, they resorted to war only when their patience was exhausted by the will of the Colonists who tried to enforce the white man's rule without regard to the Indian's laws. The Atrocities — ??? Men's minds take queer quirks during vengeance and battle, — both sides were guilty in that respect. . . . Remember just in this era of advanced civilization, there were Buckenwald, Warsaw and Hiroshima.

*Samples of Wampanoag Baskets.  From the Haffenreffer Museum of the American Indian.*

*Photo Courtesy of Dr. J. L. Giddings, Director.*

# Chapter III

# THE MEETING

# OF THE

# CULTURES

*The statue of the great Wampanoag Sachem, today calmly surveys the traditions of the Whiteman, satisfied by the accolade the passing centuries have now bestowed on him and his people.*

*Photo by Author*

This photograph of William Allen Wall's four by seven foot oil painting depicts Gosnold and Party trading with the Wampanoags at "Smoking Rocks", a section of New Bedford, Massachusetts at the foot of Howland Street and opposite Palmer's Island. Mr. Wall's excellent portrayal was completed in 1842 and now hangs in the Old Dartmouth Historical Society and Whaling Museum in New Bedford.

# THE MEETING OF THE CULTURES

The first real facts concerning our Wampanoag Tribes came from the written accounts of early explorers who found their way to the Northeast coastal areas now known as New England. Among the earliest of these adventurers was a gentleman by the name of Verrazzano. He was a Florentine skipper, who, under the sponsorship of Frances I of Spain sailed out of Madeira in the year 1524. In a letter to the King of France after his return, he described his trip and the discovery of what is believed to be Block Island, situated in Narragansett Bay. He wrote, "We found about twenty small boats of the people which, with divers cries and wonderings, came about our ship; coming no nearer than fifty paces towards us, they stared and beheld the artificialness of our ship, our shape and apparel, then they all made a loud shout together, declaring that they rejoiced; when we had something animated them, using their gestures, they came so near us, that we cast them certain bells, glasses, and many toys, which when they had received, they looked on them with laughing, and came without fear on board our ship. . . . Their boats were made of one log, by the aid of fire and tools of stone, and of sufficient capacity to care of from ten or fifteen men. . . . They live long and are seldom sick, and if they chance to fall sick at any time, they heal themselves with fire, without any physician, and they say that they die for very age."

Professor J. Lewis Diman wrote some historical sketches of his native town of Bristol, R. I., entitled "Annals of Bristol" published in 1845-6. In this he mentions a visit by Thorfinn, an early Norseman, whom he believed visited these shores of New Eng-

57

land in the years 1000-1007 bringing with him three
ships and 160 men. Professor Diman concluded this
particular account saying, "The only trace which has
been left by the Northmen, of their wintering in
Bristol, is a rock situated near the Narrows. This
was said to have been cut with characters in an
unknown tongue, but was unfortunately destroyed
by a heedless hand. This circumstance can never
cease to be regretted."

However, this rock has been re-discovered and
now lies upon the shore of the farm once belonging
to Dr. Charles H. R. Doringh, between Mount Hope
and the Narrows. It is believed that these Norsemen
were the first White Men the Wampanoags ever saw.

It is also a matter of recorded history that Bar-
tholomew Gosnold sailed into the shores of Buzzards
Bay and explored the Island of Cuttyhunk which
now has a town by name of Gosnold. This Island
of the Elizabethan group was discovered by him in
the year 1602. It is believed that it was he that
named the largest Island of this group, Martha's
Vineyard. Roger Williams first referred to it as,
Martin's Vineyard.

The next explorer of record credited with having
visited these localities also landed on the Vineyard.
His name was Samuel Champlain. He was on an
expedition sanctioned by France in the year 1606.

In the year 1614, Captain Adrian Block (of Block
Island namesake), a Dutch explorer visited this same
group of islands.

The celebrated Captain John Smith of Pocahontas
legend made a voyage in the year 1614, and it is
said that he landed on Cape Cod in the vicinity of

the Nausett Indian country. It is also known that a Captain Hunt, who sailed under Smith's command, visited the Elizabethan Islands and mingled with the tribes on Martha's Vineyard in the year 1615.

Although some historians say that Sir Frances Drake stopped at Cape Cod in the year 1586 and made contact with the Indians on the mainland, it is believed that the first Englishman known to have visited Massasoit, Sachem of the Wampanoag Federation, was a Captain by name of Thomas Dermer. In the year 1619, he did write an account of his explorations about the shore and on to the land occupied by the Wampanoags. He said that he found places which had been inhabited, but he saw no evidence of living people. He believed that a great sickness was befalling the people and wiping out the tribes.

He mentioned stopping at Patuxet, (the spot where the Pilgrims later settled), where he found all the people dead. He had with him the Indian, Squanto, who was believed to be returning to his native tribes; hence the stop at Patuxet where Squanto had lived previous to his capture and shipping to England.

Then traveling overland into the forest, Dermer moved westward into the Nemasket country, which is now the town of Middleboro, Mass. From that point he sent a message to Massasoit.

In this expedition, the Captain reclaimed two Frenchmen, who had been shipwrecked off the coast and had been cared for by the Indians for three years.

We will now quote from Captain Dermer's own account, "When I arrived at my savages' (referring to Squanto) native country, finding all dead, I traveled alongst a day's journey, to a place called Nemasturghurt (Nemasket) where, finding inhabitants, I dispatched a messenger a day's journey farther West to Pokonokit, which bordered on the sea, whence came to see me two kings, attended with a guard of fifty armed men, who being disireous of novelty, gave me content in whatsoever I demanded, where I found that former relations were true."

Historians believe that these two kings mentioned in Dermer's story, were none less than Massasoit and his brother, Quadaquina.

The Captain in his account states that he believed that the Indians might have killed him at Nemasket had it not been for his guide, Squanto. (Squanto was one of the five natives kidnapped from the coast of New England in the year 1615 by a Captain George Weymouth who was sent here by England in search for a Northwest Passage.)

In the year 1620, in the month of September, particularly on the sixth day, there commenced a voyage and events that were destined to affect the lives of every Wampanoag Indian in the Pokanoket Country. It was on this day that the Pilgrims set sail from Plymouth, England, in their ship "Mayflower" in search for a new home.

Most of us are acquainted with the story of the Pilgrims and their voyage and ultimate settlement at Plymouth; and we, therefore, will not take into account the story of the Pilgrims except in that respect where actual contact with the Wampanoag tribes is concerned.

After a stormy and hazardous crossing, they arrived at Cape Cod on November 11, 1620 and anchored the Mayflower in Provincetown Harbor.

It was Captain Miles Standish and a well-armed group of sixteen men who first ventured on to the land; setting foot from their shallop on the shores of the locality now known as Eastham, Mass., in the Nausett Indian country.

They first saw the Indians as they ran into the woods obviously frightened by so formidable a force as that of Miles Standish. The noble captain was very anxious to make contact with these aborigines, so he followed their tracks inland and camped in the forest overnight. On the next day he came to a fresh water pond, where he noticed worked ground where the Indians planted their vegetables. Walking on into the woods they came upon heaps of sand and after investigation, they found therein stores of grains, beans, corn, etc. They gathered a few seeds for planting and returned to the Mayflower.

A few days later Miles Standish and a group of thirty Pilgrims went on to shore and resumed their reconnaisance where they found several deserted villages left in a state to suggest abandonment.

The famous "First Encounter" between the Pilgrims and the Indians, describes the first attack made upon Miles Standish and his group by the Nausett Indians. This first entanglement with the aborigines was of short duration and of no serious consequence, for once the Pilgrims' muskets were fired, the Indians retired in great haste.

It was noticed by the Pilgrims that during the first weeks, the Indians continued scouting around the settlement at Plymouth, but none dared show himself until March of the following year. At one time the settlers missed some tools which they knew had been stolen by the Indians.

In March, 1621, the event of the now famous visit of Samoset took place. Walking boldly down Leyden Street, much to the amazement of the Pilgrims, Samoset came and spoke to the white men saluting them with the words "Welcome Englishmen."

Samoset's home was in the section of Maine that is now called Kennebec County, and it is not hard to imagine that Massasoit, after having been informed of the strange white settlers in his land, called upon Samoset knowing that he spoke the white man's tongue.

Samoset was described as being a very handsome Indian, tall and erect. His face was painted with red and black lines. In his long black hair he had braided three eagle feathers. He carried a long bow and there was a quiver of arrows slung over his shoulders.

He told them that he had learned his English from the men who had come to fish off the shores of the coast of Maine not far from the section now called Rockland. He was one of the chiefs of the Monhegan Tribe and had been eight months in the Pokanoket country, which was but a day's sail from his home, but five day's journey over land. He told them that he had a friend named Squanto who knew how to speak English better than he as he had lived in England for three years. The Pilgrims were of course very curious to learn the strength of the various tribes thereabouts, and they asked him, "as also of ye people hear, of their names, number, and strength; of their situation and distance from this place, and who was chief among them."

Samoset told them the place on which they had settled was known as Patuxet, and that a great plague several years before had killed off all the inhabitants. He said that there were still many Indians in the forest beyond them and that soon they would come and trade and bring furs. He told them that the Indians were great hunters, as, "white man not know how to make good traps like Indian." It was very chilly that day and due to his scanty dress, they offered him a horsemen's coat, and then sat down to listen to more of his stories.

Samoset requested some beer, but they offered instead, whiskey, bisquits, butter, and cheese pudding and a piece of black mallard duck, which he ate with relish, having been accustomed to the white man's food.

As night came, Samoset still lingered on and with a little reluctance the leaders pondered where to lodge him. They finally decided to offer him quarters at the home of Stephen Hopkins wherein he refused a bed, preferring to lie on the floor by the fire-place. On the next day Samoset was given presents and he left Plymouth promising to return with some of his Wampanoag friends.

On Sunday (which was the next day) he again appeared, with five stalwart friends. During the first day of conversation the Pilgrims had mentioned that they had missed some of their tools. It is interesting to note that this group brought back the tools with their heartfelt apologies. They in turn wanted to trade with the Pilgrims on that day, but it being Sunday, the pious Pilgrims refused, and asked them to come for such business on the morrow.

On March 22, 1621, occurred the next important meeting between the settlers and the Wampanoags. Samoset returned on this day with Squanto, the friend he had spoken about, whom he said spoke better English than he. They carried with them skins and dried herrings as gifts. They also brought with them the news that their great Sachem, Massasoit, leader of all the Wampanoag tribes, was in the locality, together with Quadequina, his brother, and a group of sixty of their men; and desired to speak with the Pilgrim leaders.

For an interesting account of this meeting by an eye-witness we quote from a story in "Mourt's Relations" edited in 1865 by Henry M. Dexter. "The 22nd of March, 1621, was a very fare warme day, about noone we met again about our publique businesse, but we had scarce been and houre together but Samoset came again, and Squanto, the only native of Patuxet, where we now inhabite, who was one the twentie captives that by Hunt were carried away, and had beene in England Y dwelt in Cornehill with Master Slanie, a Merchant, and could speak a little English, with three others, and they brought with them some few skinnes to trucke, and some red Her-rings newly taken and dried, but not salted, and signified unto us, that their great Sagamore, Massasoyt — was hard by, with Quadequina his brother, and all their men. They could not well express in English what they would, but after an houre the King came to the top of a hill over against us, and had in his trayne sixtie men, that wee could well behold them, and they us; we were not willing to send our governour to them, and they unwilling to come to us, so Squanto went againe unto him, who brought word that wee should send one to parley with him, which we did, which was Edward Winslow, to know his mind, and to signifie the mind and will of our governour, which was to have trading and peace with him.

We sent to the King a Payre of knives and a Copper
Chayne with a Jewell at it. To Quadequina we sent
likewise a knife and a jewell to hang in his care,
and withal a Pot of strong water, a good quantity
of Bisket, and some butter, which were all willingly
accepted. Our messenger made a speech onto him
that King James saluted him with words of love and
Peace, and did accept of him as his friend and alie,
and that our governour desired to see him and to
trucke with him, and to confirm a peace with him
as his next neighbor; he liked well of the speech and
heard it attentively, though the interpreters did not
well express it; after he had eaten and drunke himself, and given the rest of his company, he looked
upon our messengers sword and armour which he
had on, with intimation of his desire to buy it, but
on the other side, our messenger showed his unwill-
ingness to part with it; In the end he left him in the
custodie of Quadequina, his brother, and came over
the brooke, and some twentie men followed him,
leaving all their bows and Arrows behind them. We
kept six or seven as hostages for our messenger; Captain Standish and Master Williamson met the King
at the Brooke, with half a dozen Musketiers, they
saluted him and he them, so one going over, the one
on the one side, and the other on the other, conducted
him to an house then in building where we placed a
green Rugge, and three or four cushions, then in-
stantly came our Governour with Drumme and
Trumpet after him, and some few Musketiers. After
Salutations, our governour kissing his hand, the
King kissed him, and so they sat down. The
Governour called for some strong water and drunke
to him and he drunke a great draught that made
him sweate all the while after, he called for a little

fresh meate, which the King did eate willingly, and did give his followers. Then they treated of Peace, which was:

1.   "That neyther he nor any of his should injure or doe hurt to any of our people.

2.   An if any of his did hurt to any of ours, he should send the offender, that we might punish him.

3.   That if any of our Tooles were taken away when our people were at worke, he should cause them to be restored, and if ours did any harme to any of his, wee would doe the like to them.

4.   If any did unjustly warre against him, we would ayde him; if any did warre against us, he should ayde us.

5.   He should send to his neighbour Confederates, to certifie them of this, that they might not wrong us, but might be likewise comprised in the conditions of peace.

6.   And when their men came to us, they should leave their Bowes and Arrows behind them, as wee should do our Peaces when we came to them, and Lastly, that doing thus, King James would esteeme of him as friend and Allie."

To this first peace Treaty made on New England soil, Massasoit kept his word for forty years, until his death in 1661.

The Governor of Plymouth at the time of Massasoit's first visit was John Carver. He died a few weeks later. It was said that all the while Massasoit sat next to the governor, the Indian leader was shaking with fear.

The Wampanoag Sachem seemed very much pleased with the treaty as he understood it. At this meeting, he also acknowledged that the King of England would then be considered supreme owner and ruler of the Pokanoket country. As his first royal gift, Massasoit gave to the king title to all the lands that include the present towns of Plymouth, Duxbury, Carver, Kingston, Plimpton, Marshfield, Wareham, and a portion of Halifax. This was the first land title held by the Plymouth Colony.

After signing the treaty, Massasoit retired with his people and camped out in the forest about a half mile distant from Plymouth. On the next morning a group of his people came back into Plymouth and said that their Sachem desired a return visit by the English to his campsite. Captain Standish and Isaac Alderton were chosen to make this call and they were enthusiastically received by Massasoit and his followers. He gave them three or four ground nuts and some tobacco.

One morning shortly after the first day's treaty and visit, Governor Carver, noticing some of the Indians curiously lingering around the town, asked them to bring the king's kettle, which they did. The Governor filled it with peas, a gift that pleased them all very well.

Thus concludes the recorded event of the great Sachem's first visit with the Colonists. The Indians broke camp after a few days and returned to their village of Sowams, which was forty miles from Plymouth.

Close by "Plymouth Rock" at the foot of Cole's Hill the Pilgrims unload their shallop after a successful bartering trip into the Pokanoket country. In the foreground stand the friendly Wampanoags, Squanto and Hobbamock.

# Chapter IV

## MASSASOIT
## (Ousamequin)

### Great Sachem of the Wampanoags
### Protector and Preserver of the
### Pilgrims

*Massasoit's statue atop Cole's Hill in Plymouth, Massachusetts, erected by the Improved Order of Red Men in 1921 as a grateful tribute.*

*Photo by Author*

*Massasoit speaks to his people in one of their Game lodges.*
*Standing beside him are his three young sons; Moonanam.*
*Metacom, and Sunconewhew.*

# MASSASOIT

One "eye-witness" historian described Massasoit as, "In his person he is a very lusty man, in his best years, and able body, grave of countenance and spare of speech; in his attire little or nothing different from the rest of his followers, only in the great chain of white bone beads hung around his neck, and at it behind his neck, hangs a little bag of tobacco, which he drank and gave us to drink; his face was painted with a sad red like murrey, and oiled both head and face so that he looked greasily; in his bossom the king had hanging on a string a great long knife." (Drinking tobacco was the common English phrase, at the time, to express what we now call, smoking tobacco.)

Massasoit seems to have preferred to live at Sowams, a village that is believed to have been situated in the country near the present sites of Barrington and Swansea in the part now called, Warren, Rhode Island.

As, has been explained, many different spellings and names have been found for various individual Wampanoag Indians. We learned that it was their custom to change their names to correspond with great events affecting their lives.

Massasoit was first known as Ousamequin. It was derived from the Wampanoag words, Ousa, meaning yellow, and Mequin, meaning a feather. Thereby, we know that Massasoit was known originally to his people as, "Yellow Feather," one of which he wore braided in his hair.

It was not hard to assume that his name, Massasoit, came about due to the white men calling him the Indian leader, as we know, Massasoit means, "Great Leader."

At the time of Massasoit's first visit to Plymouth, it was judged that he was probably 40 years old. His death occurred in the year 1661, which was forty years after the signing of the treaty, and from these facts we conclude that he was born about 1580.

The name of Massasoit's wife was never recorded. We do know that a Wampanoag Sachem's wife held the title of, Saunks (Queen), thereby it is safe to say that she was addressed by that title.

Massasoit's immediate family was as follows:

Wamsutta was the eldest son who later became known as Alexander; Pometacom, his second son, was later called King Philip; and Sunconewhew was his youngest son. Some records state that he had two daughters, one called Mionie, and another, Amie. The daughter Amie is said to have been called such by the English, but noticing the similar sound in pronouncing "Mionie" and "Amie"; — and because there is greater credit to the belief that Massasoit had only one daughter — we feel that Amie is a corruption of Mionie, and that they are one and the same person.

Massasoit had two brothers, Akkompoin and Quadequina.

Anawon was the Federation's Missinnege (Head Panseis), and believed to be Massasoit's brother-in-law.

Quadequina, brother of Massasoit, is described in one journal as being, "A very proper, tall young man, of a very modest and seemly countenance", and was one of the tribes' esteemed men. He and his brother, Akkompoin, later became King Philip's advisors, and it is noted that Akkompoin signed many deeds and treaties. The correct Algonquin title for both of Massasoit's brothers was, Atauskawaw (Lord).

The last known family of record claiming direct kinship to Massasoit was that of Thomas C. Mitchell and wife Zerviah Gould. Mr. Mitchell died in Fall River, Massachusetts, on March 22, 1859 and his wife died several years later.

The Mitchells had eleven children; Jane W., Zerviah G., Levina C., Deloris B., Melina, Thomas C., John B., Lydia A., Emma J., Charlotte L., and Alonzo H. (Genealogy, E. W. Peirce).

The story of Edward Winslow's visit to Massasoit in July of 1621 is an exceptionally quaint and interesting account of what was actually the colonist's first attempt to explore the interior in order to gain knowledge of the Pokanoket country, and, to quote, "to apologize for some misbehaviors, to establish and to regulate an intercourse, to procure corn, and to strengthen their mutual good understanding."

Mr. Edward Winslow, and Mr. Stephen Hopkins were chosen as the ambassadors for this trip with the Indian, Squanto, as their guide. The gifts they carried with them for the great Sachem included, a red horseman's coat trimmed with white lace, a heavy copper, chain, and smaller tokens of beads, etc. They set out on foot on July 3, 1621 and by three o'clock in the afternoon of the same day arrived at the Indian village of Nemasket (now the site of Middleboro, Mass.), where they were received with genuine pleasure. The Indians at this village offered the travelers food which consisted of a very special Indian bread called Mozium, and made of Indian corn, and a serving of the eggs of Shad (fish) boiled in a stew of ground acorns.

After leaving Nemasket they next came upon the Titicut River (now Taunton River) where they met up with a friendly party of Nemasket Indians busily fishing upon a weir for bass, which they were catching in abundance. The three emissaries encamped here for the night, and on the next morning just after breakfast, accompanied by six of their new-found friends, Winslow and his party traveled six miles along the banks of the river to a shallow point where Squanto knew there was an easy fording place.

As they attempted to cross the river, they were met by two strange Indians who did not recognize them and demanded to know the identity of Winslow's party. Upon identification, the two Indians apologized, and offered what food they had with them.

Despite the heat of the day, it was remarked that they found no difficulty in finding drinking water, as the route abounded with frequent cool springs of fresh water. At another point of their travels they came upon an Indian and two squaws who were fishing on the banks of a salt marsh. In their baskets they had roasted crabs and other shell fish, which were offered to the travelers. The shellfish dug up by these fisherman included oysters, clams and quahogs.

A few miles farther on they arrived at Mettapoiset village, (now Gardiner's Neck in Swansea), where they were again cordially received and entertained.

The next stop was Sowams, Massasoit's village. Being absent, he was sent for, and upon his arrival our party of visitors royally saluted him with shots from their three muskets. After friendly salutations wherein it was quite evident that the chief was very pleased to see them, Winslow told him of the messages sent by the governor and their reason for coming.

Massasoit re-emphasized his intent of keeping his word as signified by the treaty and promised that all his people stood behind him to carry it through. He also promised to dispatch a quantity of seed corn to Plymouth. It was during this endorsement of his treaty at Plymouth, that Massasoit added the fact that he was leader of 30 tribute tribes; and each in turn, he was sure, would be delighted to carry on trade with the Plymotheans. Needless to say, Massasoit was overwhelmed with the horseman's coat and chain, and lost little time in proudly displaying them to all assembled. Mr. Winslow's own account of the rest of this visit as recorded in Morton's Relations best describe it as, "Late it grew but victuals he offered us none; for indeed he had not any, being he came so newly home. So we desired to go to rest. He laid us on the bed with himself and his wife, they at the one end and we at the other, it being only planks a foot from the ground and a thin mat upon them. Two more of his chief men, for want of room, pressed by and upon us, so that we were worst weary of our lodging than of our journey.

"The next day being Thursday, many of their Sachems or Petty governors came to see us, and many of their men also. About one o'clock Massasoit brought two fishes that he had shot; they were like bream, but three times so big and better meat. These being boiled, there were at least forty looked for share in them, the most eat of them. This meal alone we had in two nights and a day, and had not one of us brought a partridge, we had taken our journey (homeward) fasting. Very importunate he was to have us stay with them longer. But we desired to keep the Sabbath at home, and feared we should either be light-headed for want of sleep, for what with bad lodging, the savages' barbarous singing (for they used to sing themselves to sleep), lice and fleas within doors and mosquitoes without, we could hardly sleep all the time of our being there, we much fearing if we should stay any longer, we should not be able to recover for want of strength. So that on Friday morning, before sunrising, we took our leave and departed, Massasoit being both grieved and ashamed that he could not better entertain us."

On their return journey to Plymouth the natives supplied them with food and, it having rained most of the trip back, they arrived home on Saturday a wet and weary trio.

Governor Bradford's account of Winslow's Journey is interesting, and we quote, "Having in some sort ordered their business at home, it was thought meete to send some abroad to see their new friend Massasoit, and to bestow upon him some gratutities to tye him faster unto them; and that also they might hereby view ye country, and see in what manner he lived, what strength he had about him, and how ye ways were to his place, if at any times they should occasion, so ye 2 of july they sent Mr. Edward Winslow and Mr. Hopkins, with ye aforesaid Squanto

for their guide, who gave him a suit of clothes, and
a horseman's coat, and some other small things,
which were kindly accepted; but they found but
short commons, and came both weary and hungry
home, for ye indians used then to have nothing
so much corn as ye had since you indians (sic)
which have stored them with their hoes, and seeing
their industry in breaking up new ground therewith.
They found his place to be forty miles from hence,
ye soil good, and ye people not many, being dead
and abundantly wasted in ye late great mortality
which fell in all these parts about three years before the coming of the Englishmen, wherein thousands of them died, they not being able to bury
one another; their skulls and bones were found in
many places lying still above ground, where their
houses and dwellings had been, a very sad spectacle
to behold. But they brought word that ye Narragansetts lived but on ye other side of that great bay, and
were a strong people and many in number, living
compact together, and had not been touched at all
with this wasting plague."

Despite the misery and tribulations of their trip,
it was a success for this pathway soon bustled with
a trade that made it the principal roadway of the
land. The Indians carried over to Plymouth nearly
all their gains of the hunt and labor. They traded
skins and furs for the implements of civilization
which had been brought to the Colonists from across
the Atlantic. A brisk business was established between London, Plymouth and Sowams. From England the men at Plymouth received cloth, coats,
hatchets, knives, kettles, hoes, plates, shoes, powder,
shot and guns, etc.

The furs and skins they traded from the Indians they sent over to London in exchange for the necessities for revitalizing and maintaining their business.

This roadway also facilitated personal access for many of the leaders to visit Massasoit. Among them were Thomas Willet, Miles Standish, and John Brown, and others of the first landowners of that period.

The story of Massasoit's illness and Winslow's visit to his sick bed is another interesting story that we will touch upon at this time.

In March of the year 1623, an Indian messenger was sent to Plymouth notifying the Governor that Massasoit was very ill and was expected to die. The urgent word sent along with this messenger was; "Chachewunnea" meaning, "he is near dead". At the same time a notice was sent that a Dutch vessel had been stranded off shore close by the Sachem's residence.

It was the custom among the Wampanoags that whenever any one of their people was sick, aid from all his friends was expected and a visit to the sick bed was prime etiquette.

Governor Bradford, realizing this custom, decided to send an official party to visit the ailing Massasoit, and at the same time to have a consultation with the occupants of the reportedly distressed Dutch vessel.

Owing to the esteem in which Massasoit held Mr. Edward Winslow, he and Mr. John Hampden, who was then visiting the colony, were asked to undertake this goodwill trip to see the sick Sachem. The good Indian, Squanto, who had acted as Winslow's guide during his first trip to Sowams, had died a few months previously. Another Indian by the name of Hobbamock went along as guide on this trip.

Winslow's account of this trip is better told in his own words: "We set forward and lodged the first night at Nemasket. The next day about one o'clock, we came to a ferry in Conbitant's country. Upon my discharging my piece, divers Indians came to us from a house not far off. They told us that Massasoit was dead and that day buried. This news struck us blank, but especially Hobbamock, who desired that we might return with all speed. I told him that I would first think of it, considering now that he being dead, Conbitant was most likely to succeed him, and that we were not above three miles from Mattapuyst, his dwelling-place.

"Although he were but a hollow-hearted friend to us, I thought no time so fit as this to enter more friendly terms with him (Conbitant) and the rest of the Sachem's thereabouts; and though it was somewhat dangerous in respect of our personal safety, because myself and Hobbamock had been employed upon a service against him which he might fitly revenge, yet esteeming it the best means, leaving the event to God in His Mercy, I resolved to put in practice if Master Hampden and Hobbamock durst attempt it with me, who I found willing so that or any other course might tend to the general good. So we went toward Mattapuyst. In the way, Hobbamock brake forth in these speeches; 'My loving Sachem, O my loving Sachem! Man have I known, but never any like thee.' And turning to me said, wilst I lived, I should never see his like amongst the Indians; saying also he was no liar, he was not bloody and cruel like other Indians, from anger and passion he was

soon recovered, easy to be reconciled toward such as
offended him; and that he governed his men better
with a few strokes than others with many; truly
loving when he loved; yea he feared we had not a
faithful friend left among the Indians; showing he
oftimes restrained their malice, etc., continuing a
long speech with signs of unfeigned sorrow.

"At length we came to Mattapuyst and went to the
Sachem's place, but Conbitant was not there but at
Puckanokick, which was five or six miles off. The
Sachem's wife gave us friendly entertainment. Here
we inquired again concerning Massasoit; that they
thought him dead but knew no certainty. Where
upon I hired one to go with all expedition to Puckanokick that we might know the certainty thereof,
and withal to acquaint Conbitant with our there
being. About half an hour before the sun setting the
messenger returned and told he was not dead, although there was no hope we should find him living.
Upon this we were much revived, and set forward
with all speed, though it was late within night ere
we got thither. When we came thither we found
the house so full of men as we could scarce get in,
though they used the best dilligence to make way for
us. They were in the midst of their charms for him,
making such a hellish noise as it distempered us
who were well, and therefore unlike to ease him
that was sick. About him were six or eight women
who chafed his arms, legs, and thighs to keep heat in
him. Having understanding left, but his sight wholly
gone, he asked who was come. They told him 'Wins-
now,' for they cannot pronounce the letter 'l', but
ordinarily use 'n' in place thereof. He desired to
speak with him. When I came to him, and they told
him of it, he put forth his hand, which I took. Then

he said twice, though very inwardly, 'Keen Wins-
now?' which is to say, 'Art thou Winslow?' I answered, 'ahhe,' that is yes. Then he doubled these
words: 'Matta neen wonchanet nanem, Winslow!'
that is to say, 'O, Winslow I shall never see thee
again.' Then I called Hobbamock and desired him to
tell Massasoit that the Governor, hearing of his sickness was sorry for the same, and though by many
businesses he could not come himself, yet he sent
me with such things as he thought most likely to do
good in this extremity, and were of if he pleased to
take I would presently give him; which he desired,
and having a confection of many comfortable con-
serves on the point of my knife, I gave him some,
which I could scarce get through his teeth. When
it was dissolved in his mouth he swallowed the juice
of it, whereat those about him rejoiced, saying that
he had not swallowed anything in two days before.
Then I desired to see his mouth which was exceedingly furred and his tongue swelled in such a manner as it was not possible for him to eat such meat
as they had. Then I washed his mouth and scraped
his tongue. After which I gave him more of the
confection, which he swallowed with more rediness.
Then he desired to drink; I dissolved some of it in
water and gave him thereof. Within half an hour
this wrought a great alteration in him in the eyes of
all that beheld him. Presently after, his sight began
to come to him, which gave him and us good encouragement. I inquired how he slept, and they
said he slept not in two days before. Then I gave
him more and told him of a mishap we had by the
way, in breaking a bottle of drink, saying if he
would send one of his men to Patuxet, I would send
for more of the same; also for chickens to make him
broth, and for other things which I knew were

good for him; and would stay the return of his messenger if he desired. This he took marvelous kindly, and appointed some, who were ready to go by two or three o'clock in the morning against which time I made ready a letter.

"He requested me the day following I would take my piece and kill him some fowl, and make him some English pottage, such as he had eaten at Plymouth which I promised. After, his stomac coming to him, I must needs make him some without fowl, before I went abroad. I caused a woman to bruise some corn and take the flour from it, and set over the broken corn, in a pipkin, for they have earthen pots of all sizes. When the day broke we went out, it being now March, to seek herbs, but could not find any but strawberry leaves, of which I gathered a handful and put into the same; and because I had nothing to relish it, I went forth again and pulled up a sassafras root and sliced a piece thereof and boiled it till it had a good relish, and then took it out again. The broth being boiled I strained it through my handkerchief, and gave at least a pint, which he drank and liked it very well. After this his sight mended more and more; also he took some rest; insomuch as we with the admiration blessed God for giving his blessing to such raw and ignorant means, himself and all of them acknowledging us the instruments of his preservation.

"That morning he caused me to spend in going from one to another amongst those who were sick in town, requesting me to wash their mouths also, and give to each of them some of the same I gave him, saying they were good folk. This pains I took with willingness, though it were much offensive to me.

"After dinner he desired me to get him a goose or a duck, and make him some pottage therewith with as such speed as I could. So I took a man with me, and made a shot at a couple of ducks, some six score paces off, and killed one, at which he wondered. So we returned forthwith and dressed it, making more broth therewith, which he much desired. Never did I see a man so low brought, recover in that measure in so short a time.

"About an hour after he began to be very sick, and cast up the broth, and began to bleed at the nose, and so continued the space of four hours. Concluding now that he must die, they asked me what I thought of him. I answered his case is desperate, yet it might be would save his life; for it ceased in time, he could forthwith sleep and take rest, which was the principal thing he wanted. Not long after his blood stayed and he slept at least six or eight hours. When he waked I washed his face, and bathed and supplied his beard and nose with a linen cloth. But on a sudden he chopped his nose in the water and drew up some therein, and set it forth with such violence as he began to bleed afresh. Then they thought there was no hope, but we perceived it was the tenderness of the nostril, and therefore told them I thought it would stay presently, as indeed it did.

"The messengers were returned; but finding his stomach come to him he would not have the chickens killed, but kept them for breed. Many wilst we were there came to see him; some by their report, from a place not less than 100 miles. To all that came, one of his chief men related the manner of his sickness, how near he was spent, how his friends, the English came to see him, and how suddenly he recovered to him this strength they saw. Upon this recovery, he brake forth into these speeches; 'Now

I see the English are my friends, and love me, and wilst I live I will never forget this kindness they have showed me.'

"Being fitted out for our return, we took leave of him; who returned many thanks to our Governor, and also to ourselves for our labor and love; the like did all that were about him. So we departed."

Massasoit was indeed very pleased and publicly announced that the Englishmen's kindness toward him at this particular time proved beyond all doubt that they were indeed great friends toward him and his tribesmen. In gratitude, before several of his panseis, he publicly told Winslow of a conspiracy against the English that was being planned by several other Indian Federations. It included the Massachusetts and Narragansetts together with some of his own tribute leaders south and west of Plymouth. (Aspinet and Iyanough.)

The Wampanoag Sachem had gained intelligence of this plot due to the fact that he was asked to join in with the conspirators. Disclosing this plan as he did, it came at a very opportune time, and the leaders at Plymouth were able to prepare themselves.

With Miles Standish and his little band of feared musketeers, the plotters were surprised into quick abandonment of their scheme. The small army engaged and killed off a few of the leaders and routed the others into the swamps of the Pokanoket country where they either starved or sneaked off farther north into the wilderness.

Once more we stress the fact that throughout all the years of relations between the Colonists and Massasoit, there is no record or instance of serious differences between them, even though it seems at times that the Pilgrims did try his patience to near the breaking point.

At one time a group of Narragansett Indians attacked Massasoit and killed one of his followers. Again this particular instance was handled by Miles Standish and his army of eight or ten men who merely fired two of their muskets and successfully ended the affair.

In the year 1639, Massasoit renewed his pledge of allegiance to the settlers at Plymouth.

The only real hostile act ever made by a white man against Massasoit occurred in 1646. At this time a blacksmith named William Cheesborough and a man named Thomas Hitt who lived in Rehoboth wantonly attacked Massasoit and other members of his tribe. The blacksmith fled into the neighboring area but was soon found and sent to prison for fourteen days, and fined six pounds. His companion, Thomas Hitt, got away with a fine of 20 shillings.

Among the visits of Massasoit to the Colonists one of the best known is, of course, that of the First Thanksgiving in the Fall of 1621. We are all acquainted with that famous story of how the governor invited Massasoit to join in his first Thanksgiving Feast. Massasoit, seemingly misunderstanding the limitations of his invitation, appeared with from sixty to one hundred of his warriors and people. With them, though, they brought fine skins and five freshly killed deer to add to the feast. These they roasted over the open fire in fair Indian style and, what with their uninhibited delight no doubt accounted for much of the success of that famous first Thanksgiving Day.

Another famous visitor to the leader of the Wampanoags came as the result of the Banishment in the year 1636 of Roger Williams. During the winter of that year records written by Mr. Williams describe his life among the Wampanoag Indians and his friendly discourses with Massasoit; "I spared no cost toward them, and in gifts to Ousamequin (Massasoit) and all his, . . . tokens and presents, . . . I was unmercifully driven from my chamber to a winter's flight, exposed to the miseries, poverties, necessities, wants, debts, hardships, of sea and land, in a banished condition. For one fourteen weeks, in a bitter winter season, I was sorely tossed and knew not what bread or bed did mean . . . my soul's desire was to do the natives good and to that end to learn their language (which I afterwards printed) and therefore I desired not to be troubled with English company . . . I was known to all the Wampanoags and the Narragansetts to be a public speaker at Plymouth and Salem and therefore with them held as a sachem. I could debate with them in their own language. I had the favor and countenance of the noble soul, Mr. Winthrop whom all Indians respected."

Roger Williams bought the Seekonk land from Massasoit and the site of Providence territory from the Narragansett chiefs, Canonicus and Miantonomo.

Throughout the years between the first meeting at Plymouth in 1621 until Massasoit's death in 1661, there was no other recorded incident of noteworthy consequence that early historians found necessary to describe about personal relations with the Wampanoag Sachem, and all other mentions deal with Massasoit's participation in transfers of various deeds of land to Whites, who beat the golden path that led to the door of his wigwam.

Long before the great Sachem's death, the Colonists controlled lands that included the towns of Bridgewater, Taunton, Rehoboth on the north; and of Sowams and Swansea on the Bay. In fact, the Colonists had moved out and practically surrounded the remaining Wampanoag villages; and no doubt seriously hindered the aborigines' way of life.

No matter, it was Massasoit who continued to sell his land and many have wondered why he did. One of the explanations of his doing so, may have been the result of his realizing his weakened national state, and of the hostility of the Massachusetts Indians on the north and the strong Narragansett tribes on the south and west.

Knowing that the Massachusetts and the Narragansetts were extremely jealous of his alliance with the English, Massasoit may have felt safer among and protected by them.

In the year 1643 Miantonomo, leader of the Narragansetts, was ordered by the commissioners of Boston to be put to death for "Malicious plots and tummults and outbreaking against Uncas, Sagamore of the Mohegans and his people, and Ousamequin (Massasoit) and his people, whose peace and lawful liberties we may not suffer to be violated . . . let Plymouth labor, by all due means, to restore Massasoit to his full liberties in respect to any encroachments by the Narragansetts or any other natives."

In 1645 the commission at Boston held another important meeting and decided it was a prime necessity to protect their friendly Indian allies, and they named Massasoit as first on their list, "but a peace well framed will hardly be secured unless either some of ye chief sachems deliver their sons as hostages or that some considerable part of the country be yielded to the English for plantations wherein there may be forts built by the English and maintained at least in part."

By the sale of Sowams (now Warren, R. I.) and its settlement by the Plymouth Colonists, Massasoit seems to have procured the best degree of protection which he and his tribe evidently needed. It is said that once under this protectorate, they enjoyed a measure of peace and quiet that they could not otherwise have had.

The deeds of transfers of lands sold by Massasoit were always signed by him or by one of his sons or counselors acting for their leader.

A Mr. John Brown bought a section now included in Taunton in the year 1640 for a very small token. Massasoit's village, Sowams, — now Warren, R. I. — was purchased in the year 1653 for 35 pounds by a Mr. James Brown, Mr. John Allen, John Hill and Mr. John Saffon and several others.

In 1661 a gentleman by the name of Thomas Willet and several others bought Rehoboth's so-called north purchases, for, "divers good causes and other valuable considerations". To give the reader an idea of the vastness of these particular tracts of land then held by the whites, we now note that it contained thirteen towns which when added to the other towns already mentioned constituted twenty municipalities; for which Massasoit received, in so far as the records obtainable show, only 200 pounds in money.

We now have insight into the manner in which Massasoit disposed of large portions of the Pokanoket country, and of the probable reason for so doing; —

and as we mentioned before, other than brief notations of land sales there are no further incidents of
interest pertaining directly to Massasoit.

Thus, in the year 1661, ended the life of Massasoit,
true friend and savior to the Pilgrims during their
most trying years.

A few years ago, an Indian grave was found and
opened at Burr's Hill in Warren, Rhode Island. Some
of the artifacts found within the grave have led some
people to believe that this was Massasoit's burial site.

All who have known and studied Massasoit's life
and character have nothing but praise toward him
and his dealings.

General Guy M. Fessenden, a famous historian,
wrote this of Massasoit, "Massasoit, though a heathen,
proved himself true to the dictates which the light of
nature suggested. He possessed all the elements of a
great mind and a noble heart. With the advantages
of civilized life and the light which pure Christianity
would have supplied, he might have achieved a brilliant destiny and occupied a high niche in the temple
of fame. In all the memorials which have come down
to us, Massasoit's character stands above reproach."

Governor Winslow wrote these words, "We have
found the Indians very faithful to their covenants of
peace with us, very loving and willing to pleasure us.
We go with them in some cases fifty miles into the
country, and walk as safely and peacably into the
woods as in the highways of England."

Here are the words of another historian named
Bicknel, "Massasoit, an Indian, a savage by birth and
inheritance though he was, will stand out in colossal
proportion as the greatest of our aboriginal Ameri-

cans, and the savior and defender of the Plymouth Colony."

In 1921, The Improved Order of Red Men erected as a grateful tribute to Massasoit, a magnificent statue of the Wampanoag Sachem. It stands on Cole's Hill in Plymouth, Massachusetts, and bears the inscription; — "Massasoit (Ousamequin) Great Sachem of the Wampanoags, Protector and Preserver of the Pilgrims."

With all this praise from eminent sources, we end our brief biography of Massasoit with this word; no doubt the hostilities of the King Philip war have been primarily responsible for the low opinion of Indian behavior passed down through all these centuries. In this matter we wish to re-emphasize the fact that we hold no prejudice. We have tried to take no sides. The facts herein compiled have necessarily been handed down by the colonists themselves, as we know the Wampanoag Indians had no way of recording such history.

This has been a work encompassing solely facts known of the Wampanoag Indian Federation, who were the friends and neighbors of the early Colonists. We hope the reader finds no partiality toward either.

In a later chapter on an attempt into a biography of Pometacom, alias King Philip, we hope to touch briefly on the acts of the war.

# Chapter V

# WAMSUTTA

## The Martyred Sachem

*This sign marks the old Indian trail and the popular route taken by both whites and red men. It was over this spot that the dying Alexander was carried to his grave.*

*Photo courtesy Howard C. Mandell*

*Alexander lies dying on the shore of the Taunton River, after a vain attempt by his wife, Weetammo, and his warriors to bring the crestfallen Sachem back home to Kickimuit following his humiliating arrest in Plymouth.*

# WAMSUTTA

Wamsutta was the eldest son of Massasoit. The date of his birth is unknown. Records show that he was first known by the name, Moonanam; but in later years it was changed to Wamsutta.

In the year 1662, he, and his brother Pometacom, went to Plymouth and professed great respect for the English and asked that English names be given to them. The court at Plymouth consented to their request and named them respectively, Alexander and Philip.

Wamsutta assumed the Sachemship of the Wampanoags upon his father's death in the winter of 1661. It is known that Wamsutta was associated with his father in the government of the Tribes for a number of years prior to Massasoit's death.

He was married to an Indian maiden by the name of Tatatanum, who later became known as Weetammo; but better known to history as the "Squaw Sachem of the Pocassets."

Alexander (Wamsutta) died in the year 1662.

It was in this year that Governor Prince of Plymouth heard rumors that Alexander was plotting a conspiracy against the settlers. The Governor sent Josiah Winslow with an armed force carrying a summons to arrest Alexander and bring him to Court to face charges for not appearing in answer to a previous request. It was said that when the Wampanoag Sachem first received the message to appear before court, he vehemently denied the plot and agreed to present himself at the appointed date but did not come. Therefore, the Winslow delegation was sent to arrest him when it was learned that he, at the

date set for the trial, was visiting the Narragansetts
whom the English supposed were arch enemies to
the Wampanoags. Hence their immediate belief in
the rumors of conspiracy.

As a result, Major Winslow set out from Marshfield
with a troop of ten men. At a point half way between Plymouth and what is now Bridgewater they
approached a large pond known as Monponsett, near
the present town of Halifax, Massachusetts. On the
shores of this pond they noticed a hunting lodge constructed in the manner befitting a kingly Indian
visitor or Sachem's hunting party and they assumed
it correctly to be Alexander's headquarters.

We quote from an early historian's ledger, "The
colonists cautiously approached and saw that the
guns of the Indians were all stacked outside of the
lodge, at some distance, and that the whole party
were in the lodge, engaged in a banquet. As the
Wampanoags were then, and had been for forty
years, at peace with the English, and as they were
not at war with any people, and were in the very
heart of their own territory, no precautions whatever were adopted against surprise."

Major Winslow dispatched a portion of his force
to seize the guns of the Indians, and with the others
entered the hut. It was a rather large building,
housing about eighty of the warriors and they showed
neither surprise nor alarm at seeing the English,
and were quite unsuspicious of what was going on.

The Major requested Alexander to come and speak
with him for a few minutes, and through an interpreter informed him of his intent. He said he was
going to take Alexander under arrest to Plymouth,
there to answer the charges of plotting against the
Pilgrims.

Naturally, upon fully understanding this mission, the Indian leader grew quite angry and made it clear that he would not submit to any such action. Whereat the Major pointed a pistol toward the breast of Alexander and said, and we quote again from the early recorder, "I am ordered to take you to Plymouth. God willing, I shall do it, at whatever hazard. If you submit peacefully, you shall receive respectful usage. If you resist, you shall die upon the spot."

The Indians were at the time all disarmed and could not resist. One can readily imagine the vexation of this proud, mild-mannered chief as he submitted to the entreaties of his followers to resort to no violence, urging him to yield to necessity. With the assurance from Major Winslow that his men would be allowed to accompany him to Plymouth, Alexander finally agreed to go.

Then with their captive, the English immediately moved back toward Plymouth. Major Winslow, realizing the heat of the day, offered his prisoner a horse; but, since he had with him his wife, Weetammo, and several other Indian women and warriors, Alexander declined the offer, preferring to walk with his people.

When the party arrived at Duxbury, Major Winslow offered the Indian King the facilities of his own home. Although he treated Alexander very courteously, he guarded him with all the vigilance he could muster until he had word from Governor Prince who was at Eastham.

It was there at Duxbury that the Wampanoag Sachem, no doubt enraged by his humiliating arrest, became very ill and suffered a very high fever. Despite the best of medical attention, his illness grew worse and worse, becoming so serious that there remained no doubt that, "The Indian warriors, gravely alarmed for their beloved chief, entreated that they might take Alexander home; promising that they would return with him as soon as he recovered. In the meantime, the son of Alexander should be sent as a hostage." The court assented to this arrangement.

The Indians took their unhappy king, dying of a crushed spirit, upon a litter on their shoulders and entered the trails into the forest. Slowly they traveled with their burden until they arrived at Titicut River (now Taunton River), where they entered on canoes.

They had not traveled far down the stream, before it became evident that their monarch was dying. They landed and placed him upon a grassy mound beneath a tall tree, and in silence the sad warriors gathered around to witness the departure of his spirit to the realms of the red man's immortality.

The fatal result of this forcible seizure of Alexander, leader of the Wampanoag Indian Federation, was indeed a tremendous blow to the Indians. It was contrary to all the considerate and peaceful atmosphere which had marked the relations between the colonists and the tribes during the life of his father, Massasoit.

The aborigines did not hide the fact that they believed their Sachem had died as the result of a shocked spirit due to his arrest. Some contended gravely that he had died from mal-treatment at the hands of the English. Weetammo fully believed that her husband was poisoned by the settlers. It is said that she, from that day on, became an avowed foe toward the white man. This feeling was unquestionably in her mind at the outbreak of King Philip's war. When she later became the Squaw Sachem of the Pocassets, she had 300 warriors at her bidding.

Excepting various visits that occurred during the transfer of deeds of land sold by Alexander, this ends the known records that enabled us to present this sketch of Wamsutta, described by witnesses as, "A noble and stalwart prince, whom by all assurances desired to follow in the footsteps of his benevolent father, Massasoit."

The name, Wamsutta, in the Wampanoag language meant, "a warm, and loving heart."

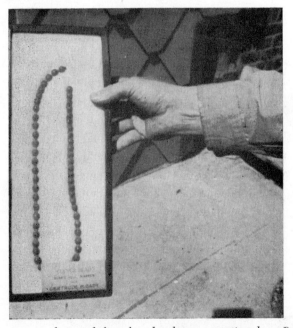

*This copper chain is believed to be the one mentioned on Page 73 — having been found in a grave said to be Massasoit's. This photo has been reproduced through courtesy of Dr. J. L. Giddings, Director of the Haffenreffer Museum of the American Indian located at Mount Hope, near Bristol, R. I.*

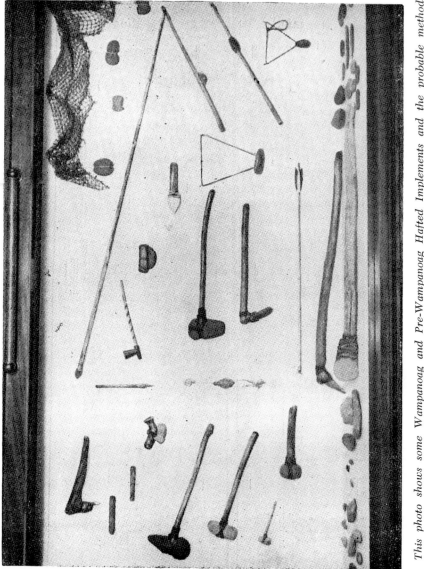

This photo shows some Wampanoag and Pre-Wampanoag Hafted Implements and the probable method of Hafting. Handles and shafts were finished with stone tools. Gut and Rawhide Thongs were used.

# Chapter VI

## WEETAMMO

### Squaw Sachem of the Pocassets

### "Bearer of the Torch"

*The road sign to the Aptucxet Trading Post, where the colonists set up a brisk trade with the Indians, situated at the west end of the Cape Cod Canal in Bourne, Massachusetts. The building has been faithfully reconstructed by the Bourne Historical Society.*

*Photo by Author*

## THE LORD'S PRAYER IN THE WAMPANOAG
## INDIAN DIALECT

"N&shun Keesukqut quttiannatanmunach k&wesunonk. Peyaum utch kukketaff &tamonk, kuttenantamoonk ne&n&nach okheit neane kesukqut. Nummeetsuongash askesutkokish assamainnean yeuyey keesukok. Kah ahquoan tamaiinnean nummatcheseongash, neane matchenenukqueagig nutaquontamounnong. Ahquc sak-ompagunnaiinnean en en gutchhuaouganit, webe phoquokwus-sinnean wuth matchitut. Newutche kutahtaunn keetass &tamonk, kah menuhkesuonk, kah sohsumoonk mickene, Amen . . ."

(The ampersand (&) represents an Indian vowel sound not reproducible then by any English letter.)

## A LITERAL TRANSLATION:

"Father ours above in heaven. Admired in highest manner be thy name. Like done thy will on earth as like in Heaven. Let us be forgiven evil doings of ours, as we would forgive wrong-doers to us. Not guide us into snares, but help us to escape from evil. Thine thy powerful kingdom, thine the strength, thine the greatest glory, Always, always wish me so. Amen."

❀      ❀      ❀

The above is the Wampanoag Dialect version of the Lord's Prayer as used in the early 17th Century by the Reverends Richard Bourne, Thomas Mayhew, Jr., John Eliot and Roger Williams in their teachings to the Wampanoag Indians of Southeastern Massa-chusetts, including Martha's Vineyard, Nantucket and Rhode Island.

# WEETAMMO

With the death of Alexander, Weetammo became widowed for a second time. Her first husband's name was Winnepurket, Sachem of Saugus, alias Wequiquinequa, and son of Nanepashemet.

It is believed that Weetammo was the daughter of one of the most powerful tribal Sagamores of the Wampanoags, Chief Corbitant of the Mettapoisets and Pocassets. The tribal lands of the Pocassets included territory now parts of Tiverton, Rhode Island and Fall River, Massachusetts.

Weetammo probably became successor to the Pocasset Sachemship due to the fact that her father left no son.

As a consequence of the serious humiliation and final arrest and death of her husband, it was natural for her to follow the fortunes of King Philip, who succeeded Alexander; and more so, when one realizes that King Philip was twice her brother-in-law, as Philip was married to her sister, Wootonekanuske.

Not long after Alexander's death, Weetammo married an Indian by the name of Quequequananachet. Later on, we read where she was married to a fourth husband, Petononowit, whom she left when he sided with the English in King Philip's war. Her fifth husband of record was a Narragansett named Quinapen, whom the English put to death in Newport, Rhode Island on August 25, 1676.

We have learned that the Indian translation for Weetammo is, "Sweet Heart" or that equivalent.

The story of Weetammo is an interesting one and from the scattered information we were able to gather, we attempt a brief sketch of her life.

Like all other Sachems of the various Tribes who had their favorite villages for the different seasons, the Squaw Sachem of the Pocassets preferred the campsite which was in the locality of the present Stone Bridge at Tiverton, Rhode Island. Her other favorite village was located between Watuppa Pond and the hills that looked down upon Mount Hope Bay, where there was in later years a village called, Indian Towne.

The first notice of Weetammo at Plymouth colony came as a result of her complaint against Alexander, then known as Wamsutta. In the year 1659 she complained that he had sold, in 1653, parcels of land which she claimed legally belonged to her, and for which she had never been paid her share. This argument was favorably adjusted by the leaders at Plymouth.

Later, other difficulties arose between Weetammo and Wamsutta. She claimed that he had again sold some land without her consent, and she went to Plymouth in June 1662, complaining of infringements of her rights in the sale of lands near Sakonnet.

One of the prisoners later taken in the King Philip War, a Mrs. Rowaldson, who later recorded a story of her capture by the Indians, had this to say of Weetammo; "Weetamore of whom I had lived and served all this while . . . a severe and proud dame was she; bestowing everyday in dressing herself near as much time as any other gentry of the land — powdering her hair and painting her face, going with her necklaces, with jewels in her ears and bracelets upon her hands . . . when she had dressed herself, her work was to make girdles of wampum and beads. . . . She had a kearsey coat covered with girdles of wampum from the loins upward . . . from her elbows to her

hands were covered with bracelets; there were hand-
fuls of necklaces about her neck and several sorts
of jewels in her ears. She had fine red stockings and
white shoes, her hair powdered and face painted red."

Captain Benjamin Church, the best known of the
Colonial leaders during the King Philip campaigns,
described a meeting with Weetammo, who was then
married to Petononowit. Captain Church was on
his way to Plymouth from a visit with another Squaw
Sachem named Awashonks.

As the Captain approached Howland's Ferry,
which connected the Town of Tiverton with Portsmouth, Rhode Island (a ferry accommodated travelers before the building of the bridge), Church met
Petononowit who was just reaching the shore in
his canoe. The Indian was returning from a visit to
Mount Hope, Philip's village.

Weetammo's husband told the Captain that he
certainly expected King Philip to declare war very
shortly. The Wampanoag Sachem was entertaining
warriors from all sections of the land. He said that
Philip had promised an attack on Sunday when the
English were at their meeting houses. Philip's first
objective was to be the burning of the white man's
houses and the killing of their livestock.

Petononowit invited Captain Church to his home,
adding that his wife was there too, not far up on
the hill. The soldier accepted the invitation, where
he found Weetammo in a sullen mood; caused, as
she put it, by the fact that all her warriors had left
her against her wishes to attend a war council with
Philip at Mount Hope. (Many writers later assumed
this attitude as a declaration that she had never
intended to side with Philip.)

In the meantime, it has been said, Philip prevailed upon Weetammo, decrying the decease of her husband, his brother Alexander, which Philip ascribed to poisoning by the English; and as later events proved, he so managed to persuade Weetammo to side with him.

Soon after the battle of July 30, 1675, when the Wampanoag Warriors escaped from a swamp and retreated into the Nipmuck territory, Weetammo's exact whereabouts were unknown for awhile. Later we learn that she joined the Narragansetts and the Wampanoags in a fort at South Kingston, at a time just before the famous swamp fight.

The next mention of the Squaw Sachem of the Pocassets records that upon her return from the Nipmuck country, she and several of her followers set up camp on the west shore of the Taunton River, not far from the present city of Fall River, Massachusetts. It was then, in the year 1675, that she left Petononowit and became the wife of Quinapen, the Narragansett Chief, whom she probably married while in the Nipmuck country. Quinapen was the nephew of the Narragansett Sachem, Miantonomo. This same Quinapen was one of the leading warriors at the famous Swamp fight, always mentioned by the students of Philip's war. He was captured on August 24, 1675, and shot by the English in Newport, Rhode Island.

As a result of the misfortunes of the war, Weetammo was forced to flee from place to place. It was in August of 1676 that an Indian traitor informed the white men at Taunton of the location of her camp, whereupon twenty soldiers succeeded in routing and capturing 36 of her people.

Weetammo managed to escape; but due to the suddenness of her flight and the lack of a canoe, she launched herself upon a crude raft and attempted to flee across the Taunton River.

Through a mishap, the raft collapsed and she was drowned. Her body was washed up on shore along the west banks of the same river near Swansea, Massachusetts.

Her body was found by the English at a point called Gardiner's Neck, then called by the Indians, Mettapoiset.

According to the custom of those days, she was beheaded, and her head was placed on a pole as an exhibition for all the good people of Taunton.

It is believed that her death occurred but six days prior to King Philip's death.

Weetammo's death was recorded by Reverend Increase Mather as follows; "Now here it is to be observed that God by himself in his own hand brought this enemy to destruction. For in that place, where the last year, she furnished Philip with canoes for his men, she herself could not meet with a canoe, but venturing over the river upon a raft, that brake unto her, so that she was drowned, just before the English found her. Surely Philip's turn will be next."

Cotton Mather offered these words, "Some Indian prisoners saw it (her head on the pole) soon after and they made a most horrid and diabolical lamentation, crying out that it was their queen's head."

We will now end this sketch of Weetammo with a description of her, given by Virginia Baker, "Her

Kingdom was but a narrow strip of Territory, Her subjects only a handful of untutored savages. But her domain was fair and fertile; her people loyal, and never was royalty worn with more royal grace, than by this dusky princess of the primeval forest."

Still another historian and noted Indian authority, Mr. Rudolph Haffenreffer, late owner of the estate which includes Mount Hope, the residence of Philip, wrote; "She lost her life in a desperate struggle for her race. She knew the pride of birth, the thrill of love, the sense of power. She lived strenuously and died struggling, perhaps the most interesting and most glorious flower of Indian womanhood."

We know that Weetammo and Alexander had at least one child, a son . . . but, aside from his being mentioned as a hostage during Alexander's arrest; there is no record of his life.

At Bourne, Massachusetts, near the western end of the Cape Cod Canal, there is a reproduction of Plymouth Colony's First Trading Post. Within this station, called Aptucxet Trading Post by the early Colonists, there is an Indian Traders Tablet placed in memory of the Indian friends and allies who lived in the territory served by the post. It is interesting to note that Weetammo's name is among them. She is listed as, "Wetamo; Squaw Sachem of Pokanoket, Consort of Wamsutta. An American queen who later bravely met inevitable death."

Other Indians honored and the tributes listed are as follows:

"Ousamequin, Massasoit, Great Sachem of the Wampanoags, For more than forty years loyal friend and ally."

"Samoset; Their first visitor, March 16, 1621. 'Welcome Englishmen', were his words of greeting. Able interpreter, guide."

"Squanto; only native of Patuxet to escape great plague of 1615-16. He directed them how to set their corne, where to fish, and also their pilot to bring them to unknown places to these parts and never left them until he died."

"Hobbamock; A Pinese, or Chief Captain, of Ousamequin. A man of Accounte for his valour — very Faithful — Constant."

"Wamsutta; Oldest son of Ousamequin. In vain he tried to prevent his brother, King Philip, from warring against the settlers."

"Tokamahamon; Appointed to the use of the colony by Ousamequin. A Special friend whom we found faithful, before and after, on all occasions."

"Quachatasset; Sachem of Manamet. Grantor of the lands of Aptucxet."

"Cawnacome; Sachem of Manamet. Signer of the Oath of Alegiance in September 1621. From him Governor Bradford bought much needed Corn during Famine 1621."

"Iyanough; Sachem of Mattachieset. Very personable, Gentle, Courteous. Indeed not like a savage, save in his attire."

"Watanamatucke. Nauquatnumack. Kanoonus, Mocrust; all Sachems of Mashpee. Keencomsett; Sachem of Mattakeese. Five trusted assistants of Richard Bourne, Preacher to the Cape division . . . ordained Minister of the Mashpees."

"Mattaquason; Sachem of Monamoyick. Grantor of lands at Nausett, 1640."

"Hiacoomes; of Nope. Devoted disciple of four generations of the Mayhews, ordained by the Apostle Eliot and Rev. John Cotton, . . . for half a century envoy of good faith and good will among his brethren of the islands."

"Nickanoose and Wanackmamak; Sachems and grantors of lands at Nantucket."

"Saul; Last of Manamets, to be buried on Indian Burial Hill at Cumassakumkanet."


## PETONONOWIT

Petononowit was Weetammo's fourth husband.

We find many corruptions of his name. He was called Peter Nunnuit by the English. We know that he was married to Weetammo and that she left him when it became quite evident that he sided with the English during the King Philip War.

History records very little of Petononowit. On May 8, 1673, he and two other Indians sold a lot of land in a section of Swansea to a Mr. Nathaniel Paine and Hugh Cole for 35 pounds and 5 shillings. In the same year it is noted that he was a witness to a dispute about land bordering the Taunton River.

By direction of the court council, in the year 1676, he, with Numpas and another Indian by the name of Issack, as his aides, was appointed inspector of Indian prisoners and held authority in the territory bounded by the "Westermost side of Sepecan River, and so westward to Dartmouth Bounds". As a result of this authority granted to him, he was known as Chief Ben Petananuett.

A strange but interesting sequel of the life of Petononowit is worthy of mention.

It is recorded that Elizabeth Pole in her 35th year (but referred to by a contemporary writer, as "that ancient dame,") purchased from Peter Nunnuit a substantial portion of the present area of the city of Taunton for "a copper pot, two iron hoes, a mirror, and a quantity of glass beads."

In the Spring of 1954, a woodchuck dug a burrow in an abandoned apple orchard owned by William H. Taylor, and located beside the Taunton River in North Middleboro, Massachusetts. Atop the mound of earth piled by the animal outside the entrance to the burrow was a portion of a human pelvis.

Mr. Taylor, as a member of the Massachusetts Archaeological Society who had participated for several years in the "dig" at Titicut, called in his associates. The material recovered as a result of their work occupies a prominent place in the Bronson Museum of the Massachusetts Archaeological Association in Attleboro, Massachusetts. It includes a copper pot, two iron hoes, a mirror and a quantity of glass beads, the latter strung with a bracelet.

There can never be a definite substantiation that the bones remaining in the grave shaft after the woodchuck had completed his home are those of Petononowit, but the correspondence of the artifacts later recovered with those paid by Mrs. Pole is so close that a careful student would be justified in claiming that a woodchuck discovered the grave of Petononowit.

## MIONIE

Before we go into an account of King Philip, we will leave the normal sequence and write a brief sketch of Massasoit's daughter, Mionie, alias "Amie." As we shall learn in a later paragraph, she no doubt is the sister mentioned as being sick by Philip as the cause of one of his excuses for not attending a meeting with the Colonists when they demanded his presence at Plymouth.

Mionie's birthday is unknown and so is the exact date of her death. We do know that she was married to Tuspaquin, the so-called "Black Sachem of the Assawompsett Tribe". He surrendered to the English and was put to death in September 1676.

Mionie and Tuspaquin had a son named Benjamin Tuspaquin who married an Indian maiden named Weecum.

Mionie's son and daughter-in-law presented her with a grandson whom they named Benjamin. This grandson's mother was the daughter of an Indian named Felix, who married Assowetough, a daughter of John Sassamon, who was once secretary to King Philip, and whose murder is believed to have been the spark that ignited the King Philip war.

Benjamin and Mercy Tuspaquin had one child named Lydia and she married an Indian named Wamsley, and they had a daughter whom they called Phoebe. She was born February 26, 1770, and died August 16, 1839. Phoebe was twice married. Her first husband was Silas Rosier, an Indian of the Marshpee Tribe. After his death, she married on March 4, 1797, a man known as Brister Gould. They had a daughter Zerviah, who was born July 24, 1805. Zerviah's husband was Thomas C. Mitchell and they were married on October 17, 1824. Mrs. Mitchell was the publisher of a book from which this genealogy was obtained.

Zerviah and Thomas Mitchell had several children whose names have been mentioned in the chapter on Massasoit. Two of these children, Wootonekanuske and Teewaleema, remained unmarried and after retiring from school teaching, moved back to the lands of their forebears. Teewaleema and his sister, who incidentally was named after Philip's wife, lived a quaint life endeavoring to the last to hold on to and revive the traditions of their ancestors. It is believed that they were the last of the royal Wampanoag blood and their remains are buried within the boundaries of the Assawompsett country. Teewaleema died in 1928.


## SUNCONEWHEW

Massasoit's third and youngest son was called Sunconewhew. It is believed that he died at a very early age because history records nothing but his name.


## QUADEQUINA and AKKOMPOIN

Since there is very little of additional interest other than what has been already said in this edition in regard to what is known of Massasoit's brothers, Quadequina and Akkompoin; — we will close these brief sketches of the Great Sachem's family with the addition of this sole fact concerning the date of Akkompoin's death. It was recorded as of July 30, 1676. He was killed by troops under the command of Benjamin Church at a spot close by the old fording log which lay for many years across a narrow strip of the Taunton River, at the spot where King Philip's wife and son were later taken prisoner. (This location is the site of the "Titicut" excavations of the Massachusetts Archaeological Society.)

*Mr. Howard C. Mandell on the famous "Sachem's Seat," said to be the ceremonial chair and favorite spot of King Philip. Located on the Haffenreffer Estate, once the site of King Philip's home at Mount Hope.*

*Photo by Author*

# Chapter VII

## KING PHILIP

### Leader of The Clash of the
### Cultures

*The Wampanoag Council Oak located at the site of the Pokanoket corn fields, now Dighton Lane in Dighton, Massachusetts.*

*Photo by Author*

# KING PHILIP

Upon the death of Alexander, the second son of Massasoit succeeded to the title of Sachem of the Wampanoag Indian Federation. This last great leader of the Wampanoags was first known as Pometacom, alias Metacom, Metacomet and Pometacomet. History records his name as King Philip.

The date of King Philip's birth is unknown and can only be guessed. The Wampanoag Indians kept no records of births or deaths.

King Philip was married to Wootonekanuske, who was a sister of Weetammo. Since history records very little of her life, we deem it appropriate to set forth now what we were able to gather about her. She being the Sachem's wife, she, of course, was addressed as Saunks.

It is known that a son was born of this union, but there is no record of his name. Nevertheless; in going over Captain Benjamin Church's account of the capture of King Philip's wife and child, we learn that in his pursuit of Philip, Church ambushed a group of Indians as they were attempting to cross the Taunton River at a point near the present Town of Middleboro, Massachusetts. Here the English soldier surprised Philip and his warriors so that the Indian was forced to flee, leaving most of his followers easy captives of the Colonist's soldiers. Among these Indian captives were Philip's wife and child.

Captain Church mentions that the boy was about nine years old. It is interesting to note that there was considerable discussion at Plymouth as to the disposition of King Philip's son. After the Court consulted with the principal reverend elders, a decision was carried, and it is believed that they indeed suffered the fate of being sold into slavery and that they lived and died on a rice plantation in the Barbados.

For a reflection of the feeling on this subject, we shall quote Judge Davis's account of the decision pertaining to King Philip's wife and son together with these words from Samuel Arnold, pastor of a church in Marshfield and John Cotton, pastor of a church at Plymouth, as written in an article dated September 7, 1676: "Upon serious consideration, we have conceived that the children of notorious traitors, rebels and murderers, especially of such as the principal leaders and actors in such horrid villanies, and that against a whole nation, yea, the whole Isereal of God, may be involved in the guilt of their parents, and may, be adjudged to death, as to us seems evident by the scriptures instances of Saul, Archam, Haman, the children of whom were cut off by the sword of justice for the transgressions of their parents, . . ."

Unfortunately, the recorded history of King Philip lies in the collections of articles written on King Philip's War of which he was the prime actor and accused instigator.

In attempting this work on the Wampanoag Indian Federation we had no desire to delve further into the events of that war and preferred to gather brief sketches of the various tribal members of the Wampanoags. Nevertheless; it is practically impossible to gain an insight into any account of Philip's dealings without the taint of the battles with which he is associated.

Therefore, after setting forth a few of the events that we were able to find that directly concerned

Philip previous to the war, we will attempt a brief synopsis of the "Clash of the Cultures" as taken from the writings of Captain Benjamin Church, who was the most celebrated soldier of that Indian War, and the writings of Mr. George N. Bodge. For interesting accounts of King Philip's war, we refer the reader to "The History of King Philip's War", by Benjamin Church; and "Soldiers of King Philip's War", by George N. Bodge.

King Philip's Indian name as recorded by the early historians takes on many different spellings, all stemming out of the phonetic sound similar to that of "Metacom" and "Comet". We accept the most widely used, Pometacom, as it was his tribal name.

We know how he and Alexander requested the change of name when Pometacom accepted the English name of Philip. The "King" came about later when he was leader of the Wampanoags and refused to deal with the Governor because Philip learned that the Pilgrim leader was subject to the King of England; and Philip felt that he, being a King, should deal with none less than the English King.

One of the older New England historians, Mr. Hubbard, said; "For his ambitious and haughty spirit, he was nicknamed King Philip."

King Philip chose as his chief village the section of his territory called (Montaup) Mount Hope now situated in Bristol, Rhode Island, on the west shores of the bay that bears the same name. It is believed that the name Mount Hope is an English corruption of the last two syllables of the Wampanoag word Uppaquontup, meaning, "at the high place, or, the head."

Students who have delved into the stories of King Philip's life all agree that he nursed hostile feelings toward the English from a very early age. It is a noted fact that immediately upon his attaining control of the tribes, plots and rumors of conspiracy ran rampant throughout the colonies.

No matter, despite this feeling of animosity, we do know through early records that he continued to sell to the white man large portions of his country which he had inherited from his father and brother.

In 1662 several settlers who lived in Dedham bought from Philip a tract of land that lay within the bounds of Wrentham paying him 24 pounds 10 shillings.

In 1668 a Mr. Constant Southworth and divers others acquired from King Philip all the meadow lands from Dartmouth to Mattapoisett. The price for this tract was set at 15 pounds.

We also learned that a Mr. Thomas Weld purchased from the Sachem all the lands between the Wannascottaquett and Cawatoquissets Rivers. This land was said to be two miles long and one mile in width, and cost Mr. Weld ten pounds sterling. The deed was witnessed by Philip's counsellors, Tom and Nannutnew.

The Wampanoag Sachem also sold in 1668, tracts of land now included in the section around Swansea, Massachusetts. In 1669 more lands located near Swansea were also conveyed to the white man. In 1670 he sold five hundred acres in the same area for 20 pounds.

In 1669 Mr. John Cook purchased a tract of land located near the village of Nokatay for 10 pounds.

About the same time Philip disposed of a large tract within the boundaries of Middleboro for 13 pounds.

In 1671 a deed signed by Philip and Monyocam transferred, for five pounds, some land lying near Acashewah in Dartmouth. The buyer in this instance was a Mr. Hugh Cole of Swansea.

For a tract of land containing twelve square miles, and located just south of Taunton, Philip received 143 pounds from a Mr. William Brenton and others. This particular transfer was made in 1672.

We learn by the records that Philip continued to sell large tracts of land, seemingly unmindful of the vise he himself was tightening around his country. We do know that eventually he awoke to circumstances, for it was not long before he summoned a council of war amongst his tribes.

At this meeting he dwelt on the life of the Wampanoags before the English came, and on the constant encroachment upon their way of living. He saw that the English were indeed driving his tribes and all Indians into complete submission to the white man's way of life. He also must have spoken of the kindness of his beloved father, Massasoit, toward the early settlers. The untimely death and humiliating treatment of his brother Alexander must have bred a dire hatred toward the Colonists.

Thoughts of the sudden betrayal and death of Miantonomo, of the Narragansetts, at the hands of the whites may also have nourished further resentment of an example of treatment to be expected by all Indians. All of these harbored grievances unquestionably were built up at the war council in the picturesque and dynamic discourse that only the Indian leaders were capable of delivering to their people. We know of this council as a result of the disclosure made by Petononowit. We also know that the end result was a declaration of war against the whites.

No more were they to be at the beck and call of the settlers. No more were they to humble themselves in servitude. This was to be the "show down". This was the inevitable "Clash of the Cultures"!

Rumors of the impending strife surreptitiously traveled from one settlement to another, but little action was taken by the leaders at Plymouth.

Finally, in August in the year 1662, Philip appeared at Plymouth to clear himself of charges made against him. At the court he denied the charges of a conspiracy, and earnestly requested the continuance of the peace and friendship that had existed so long between the English and the Wampanoags. Accordingly, a treaty was drawn up, on which he set his mark and the sign of his uncle Akkompoin. This treaty was also witnessed by the Indian John Sassamon (then Philip's secretary), together with the marks of Francis, Sachem of Nanset; Nimrod, alias Pumpasa; Punckquaneck, and Aquetequesh.

As early as 1671, the government at Plymouth became very anxious about the apparent influence that Philip seemed to be gaining over all the Algonquin tribes, and sent a command to him to come to Taunton and explain his conduct. As recorded by Mr. Abbot; "He was yet unprepared for war, and was very reluctant to precipitate hostilities, which he had sufficent sagacity to foresee would involve him in ruin, unless he could first form such a coalition of the Indian Tribes as would enable him to attack all the English settlements at one and the same time. At length, however, he found that he could no longer refuse to give some explanation of the measures he was adopting, without giving fatal strength to the suspicions against him. Accordingly, on the 10th day of April of 1671, he took with him a band of warriors, armed to the teeth, and painted and decorated with the most brilliant trappings of barbarian splendor, and approached within four miles of Taunton. Here he established his encampment, and with native punctiliousness, sent a message to the Plymouth Governor, informing him of his arrival at that spot, and requiring him to come and treat with him there. The Governor, either afraid to meet these warriors in their own encampment, or deeming it beneath his dignity to attend the summons of an Indian Chieftain, sent Roger Williams, with several other messengers, to assure Philip of his friendly feelings, and to entreat him to continue his journey to Taunton, as a more convenient place for their conference. Philip, with caution, which subsequent events proved to have been well-timed, detained these messengers as hostages for his safe return, and then, with an imposing retinue of his painted braves, proudly strode forward toward the town of Taunton. When he arrived at a hill upon the outskirts of the village, he again halted, and warily established sentinels around his encampment.

"The Governor and magistrates of the Massachusetts Colony, apprehensive, it would seem, that the Plymouth people might get embroiled in a war with the Indians, and anxious, if possible, to avert so terrible a calamity, had dispatched three commissioners to Taunton, to endeavor to promote a reconciliation between the Plymouth Colony and Philip.

These commissioners were now in conference with the Plymouth court.

"When Philip appeared upon the hill, the Plymouth magistrates were quite eager to march and attack him, and take his whole party prisoners, and hold them as hostages for the good behavior of the Indians. With no little difficulty the Massachusetts commissioners overruled this rash design, and consented to go out themselves and persuade Philip to come in and confer in a friendly manner upon the adjustment of their affairs.

"Philip received the Massachusetts men with reserve, but with much courtesy. At first he refused to advance any farther, but declared that those who wished to confer with him must come where he was. At length, however, he consented to refer the difficulties which existed between him and the Plymouth Colony, to the Massachusetts commissioners, and to hold the conference in the Taunton meeting-house. But, that he might meet his accusers upon the basis of perfect equality, he demanded that one-half of the meeting-house should be appropriated exclusively to himself and his followers, while the Plymouth people, his accusers, should occupy the other half. The Massachusetts people, three gentlemen, were to sit alone, as umpires. We can but admire the character of Philip as presented in these arrangements."

King Philip insisted that he was not arming against the English, but as a precaution against attack from the Narragansett Tribes. He did accuse the English of depredation upon his corn fields.

The crafty white leaders contradicted his stories with such proofs that they completely befuddled

Philip; whereupon he confessed the whole conspiracy.

We quote again from the records of that event, ". . . that it was the naughtiness of his own heart that put him upon that rebellion, and nothing of any provocation from the English."

He signed another agreement offering to submit all the firearms acquired by his people. This he did not do; and the Plymotheans sent a complaint to the government at Boston informing them that Philip did not submit his guns as he had agreed. Through some preconceived plan, or by coincidence, Philip arrived at Boston at the same moment as the messenger carrying the Plymouth complaint. At Boston Philip made a favorable impression in regard to the matter, and a good report was sent back to Plymouth.

Nevertheless, it was planned at that time to convene a general congress of leaders from all the Colonies to meet at Plymouth and settle affairs with Philip. At this meeting held in September, 1671, Philip confessed himself as the instigator, and stipulated payment of a fine of the equivalent of one hundred dollars to offset the expense to which he had put the colonies. Among the covenants also promised was the delivery of five wolves' heads, (if it was possible for him to get), or as many as he could get until they came to five wolves' heads each year.

Seemingly, peace was restored for the next few years.

We know that Philip continued to hold many court councils with his tribes. One of his favorite meeting spots was in the locality of the present site of

Dighton, Massachusetts, where an old and magnificent oak tree still stands. It is called the "Council Oak" and was known to the earlier residents of Dighton, as the "Charter Oak". This tree still lives as an impressive memorial marking a spot in the center of the Pokanoket Corn Fields where King Philip, and probably Massasoit before him, held conferences with their sagamores.

The trunk of this massive white oak is nearly six feet in diameter. Its large horizontal branches span a circle ten or twelve times that much. It is certainly more than 500 years old.

It may be reached by driving westerly from Elm Street, up Dighton Lane, a narrow dirt road across a small plain which has been planted with corn and other crops for more than three hundred years.

Through the months, Philip continued calling the Miawenes (councils), and in 1674 the pot boiled over and disaster poured forth in all its fury. It is believed that the first real act of hostility in the war occurred as a result of the murder of John Sassamon by the Indians.

John Sassamon was a Massachusetts Indian who was born in the neighborhood of Dorchester. He was converted, and was educated and became a school teacher at Natick. It is said that he helped John Eliot in the preparation of the Indian Bible, but it is known that he once gave up the faith and returned to the Indians where be became a valuable aid and secretary to King Philip. After a few years with Philip, Sassamon left Mount Hope and turned again to the Christian Faith. He settled in the Nemasket area where he became a teacher to the Indians. The Assawompsett Chief, Tuspaquin, gave him and his son-in-law each a house lot. Sassamon introduced the cranberry to the settlers.

Records state that Sassamon revealed Philip's final plot to the government at Plymouth. On January 29, 1675 he was found dead beneath the ice at Assawompsett Pond near the present site of Lakeville, Massachusetts. Later, three Indians by the name of Tobias, and his son Wampapaquam, and Mattashunannonma, were tried by a jury of twelve white men and eight Indians. They were found guilty of John Sassamon's murder, but the court left no doubt that it had occurred by Philip's command.

This event took on the proportions of the first great trial held in New England by an English court. For the sake of record we found the name of the white jurors listed as, William Sabine, William Crocker, Edward Sturgis, William Brookes, Nathaniel Winslow, John Wadsworth, Andrew Ringe, Robert Vixon, John Done, Jonathan Bangs, Jonathan Shaw, and Benjamin Higgins. The Indian jurors chosen were Maskippague, Hannoo, George Wampye, Acannotus and another by name of Ope.

This trial and its result enraged Philip. He concluded that the Indian no longer would be allowed to carry on his own government in his own way. With terrible fury he began the burning of isolated settlements and the killing of the white man's livestock.

King Philip's war had begun! This was to be the showdown between the Indians and the whites. It was inevitable that one or the other would be the sole survivors.

The rest is history and a voluminous story in itself; and again we state that those interested in accounts of this Indian War should avail themselves of the many excellent editions that deal with these campaigns in a detailed manner.

The following cursory account is taken from the detailed descriptions of the Church and Bodge accounts, and may give the reader an insight into a portion of the campaigns.

It was known that the Narragansett Indians were not ready to enter the war at the time. They were to have furnished King Philip with four thousand warriors; but it was not long before Philip managed to persuade them to come to his assistance.

The first Indian attack was made upon the settlement of Swansea. This occurred on the 24th of June, 1675. Indians had ambuscaded the settlers as they were returning from a prayer meeting on a fast day, and killed several of them.

Cotton Mather relates, that: "In a still, shiny morning, there were divers persons in Malden, who heard in the air, on the southeast of them, a great gun go off, and presently thereupon the report of small guns, like musket shot, very thick, discharging as if there had been a battle. This was a time when there was nothing visible done in any part of the colony to occasion such noises. But that which most of all astonished them was the flying of bullets, which came singing over their heads, and seemed very near to them; after which, the sound of drums passing along westward was very audible; and, on the same day, in Plymouth Colony, in several places, invisible troops of horses were heard riding to and from."

The attack and abandonment of Swansea was followed in a few days by further Indian massacres at Taunton, Middleboro and Dartmouth.

The Colonists immediately flew to arms.

On June 15, 1675, Benjamin Church, then residing in the vicinity of Little Compton in the country of the Saghonett Tribe, secured a promise from Awashonks, the Squaw Sachem of that tribe, a promise whereby she said that she would side in with the English against King Philip.

Soon after his meeting, Captain Church left to report the alliance to the government at Plymouth. It was during this trip that he was hailed by Petononowit (Weetammo's husband), and was invited to visit them at their lodge in the vicinity of the present Stone Bridge Inn at Tiverton, Rhode Island.

While at Plymouth, Benjamin Church disclosed Awashonks' promise and also the news of King Philip's war council as told to him by Petononowit and Weetammo. It was just a few days after this meeting with the Plymouth government that the Indians attacked Swansea.

On June 21st, the Governor ordered the Captains of the various towns to march that day towards Plymouth to give their assistance.

On June 22, 1675, Church led a party of English and friendly Indians ahead of the main army to Brown and Myles' Garrison. On June 24th, the first blood in King Philip's war was shed at Swansea, near the present city of Fall River, Massachusetts.

June 28, 1675, there was a skirmish at Miles' Bridge in which William Hammond was killed. Near the end of June the same year, troops marched from Mount

Hope Neck into Kickimuit. Through error they fired upon each other, resulting in the wounding of an ensign by the name of Savage. It was here that they found eight beheaded Englishmen whose heads had been stuck on poles and staved into Philip's drums. (By this time the Wampanoags had adopted the use of drums.)

In July of 1675, the English began the construction of a fort at Kickimuit. On July 7, Captain Church and a small party proceeded over the Bristol Ferry into Rhode Island by way of Pocasset. It was on July 9th of that same year they encountered a group of Indians in a Pea field in the vicinity of Portsmouth, Rhode Island, and a running battle took place between the two small forces with no resulting casualties. Shortly afterward, Church heard that Weetammo was in the locality and started after her, but she managed to elude him.

On July 15, 1675, the Colony's forces moved from Mount Hope Neck Fort to Rehoboth from whence they went to Gardiner's Neck, then on to Taunton. On July 19th, they had their first encounter with Philip. After a march to Pocasset, where they believed they had Philip trapped in a marsh, the Wampanoag Sachem managed to escape through their lines by use of rafts floating quietly and unseen over the murky water and onto the Taunton River, wherein Philip disappeared into the Nipmuck Indian Country.

About this time in July, the settlement of Acushnet (then in Dartmouth territory) was destroyed by the Indians. Although Apponagansett was also burned, local settlers were saved at Russell's Garrison which withstood an attack on the approximate day (July 29 or 30).

During this month another fort was built at Pocasset. It was during this humid time of year that the English troops provided themselves with the improved security of this fort. At the same time it is believed that the Indians spent the remainder of the summer consolidating their forces and recruiting in the Nipmuck country and as far west as the section now Albany.

On December 10, 1675, Captain Church started for Boston with Governor Winslow on an expedition against the Narragansett Indians. They arrived at Miles Garrison in Rehoboth on that same day. December the 11th, Captain Church and Richard Smith traveled over by way of ferry into Wickford, Rhode Island territory and surprised 18 of the enemy, whom they proudly presented to the Governor on that very same night.

December 12th found the company being fortified by the addition of Massachusetts and Plymouth Troops who had been marching around the country. They arrived in time to assist, on December 14th, in two forays that resulted in nine Indians killed, twelve taken prisoners, and 150 wigwams burned.

Several stragglers from the main body of the English were cut off on December 15th. On the 16th, Captain Prentice with his troops of horse went down to Pentequamscut and found that the Indians had burned Bull's Garrison, killing ten men and five women and children.

December 17, 1675, the Connecticut troops arrived at the ruins of Bull's Garrison; and on the next day the Massachusetts and Plymouth troops marched over and joined them at 5 p.m.

At about 1 p.m. on December 19th they convened on the edge of the swamp where the famous Narragansett fight took place, and fierce action began. It was during this battle that Captain Church was wounded along with several other Englishmen. It was bitterly cold, and snow was falling during this swamp fight. Although the Colonists' army suffered greatly, their victory here proved the decisive factor in the Indians' ultimate defeat.

Captain Belcher later mercifully arrived nearby with a vessel loaded with much-needed provisions. Following this bitter battle late in December the wounded Captain Church and others were carried over into Rhode Island, but Massachusetts and Plymouth troops remained, and were later reinforced.

On January 27, in 1676, the Connecticut forces arrived at Wickford, Rhode Island, and an army of 1600 troops headed for the Nipmuck Indian country. On January 28, they attacked Pumham's Village located in the area that is now Warwick, Rhode Island.

Between February 1st and 7th in the year 1676, the army was forced to return home for want of provisions. On February 10th the Indian massacre of Lancaster occurred; and on February 21st Medfield was leveled by Indian fires.

A Plymouth Council of War was called on February 29, 1676, and met at Marshfield. Church advised the sending of 300 soldiers, one-third to be friendly Indians; but the council did not take his advice.

From March 8th to the 11th, Captain Church moved his family from Duxbury to Rhode Island. It was on March 12th, that the Indians attacked Clark's Garrison in Plymouth and destroyed it.

During the period from the 16th to the 26th of the same month, the settlers at Rehoboth were attacked and the town was burned. On April 21, Captain Wadsworth and his company were swallowed up at Sudbury.

On May 19, 1676, Captain Turner surprised the Indians at the great falls of the Connecticut River, but was himself killed.

On June 6th, Captain Church arrived at Plymouth and met with the General Court; and later received permission to return to his family at Rhode Island. His route was by shallop, leaving from what is now Wood's Hole and sailing along the Islands of Pasque, Naushon and Cuttyhunk, thence across the Bay directly toward Sakonnet Point, where he spied some Indians fishing for Tautog off the so-called Onion Rock, that still is to this day a favorite spot for Tautog fishing.

After hailing the Indians from a distance and being recognized by them, Church learned they were Awashonks' people; whereupon he asked them to take word to their queen, informing her that he desired a conference with her. The Indians complied with his request and Church immediately set out for Newport, Rhode Island to get permission from his superiors to speak at the conference with their authorization.

On June 10th, Captain Church sailed across the Bay with Daniel Wilcox to a rendezvous at the "Treaty Rock" and met with the Squaw Sachem of the Saghonates.

On June 21st the Plymouth Army was alerted to start for Taunton.

On the 25th of June, after having secured further assurances from Awashonks that she would assist the whites in their battles with King Philip, Peter, her son, was sent as a messenger from Rhode Island to Plymouth to carry the word of the renewed alliance.

During the day of June 26th, the Colony's army arrived again at Pocasset, where Captain Church went to meet with Major Bradford.

Captain Church returned on the 28th to Awashonks' camp and told her of the arrival of the Colonist's army. . . . He saw her and left instructions, as he was ordered, and returned to Major Bradford.

It was on this same day that Peter Awashonks and his two Indian companions appeared before the court at Plymouth and related Awashonks' submission to the English. On June 29th, of this fatal year of 1676, the army marched down to Punkatese, where Captain Church decided to go over to Sakonnet and see Awashonks again. He asked her to come with him to Punkatese and formally submit to Major Bradford, who ordered the Indian Sachem and her people to report to Sandwich six days from then.

Awashonks agreed to meet Captain Church there within a week.

On July 1st of the same year, the army traveled back to Pocasset and over to Mount Hope, and barely missed another engagement with a group of Indians who were busy digging clams at Wepoiset.

On July 6th, the army having got comfortably back to Miles' Garrison, Captain Church secured leave to keep his promise with Awashonks and the Saghonates at Sandwich.

The Captain arrived at Plymouth on July 7th, and on the same afternoon started for Sandwich. It was also on this day that Major Bradford's army marched after Philip.

July the 8th found Captain Church arriving at the present locality of Mattapoisett, Massachusetts where he found Awashonks and her tribe happily fishing and feasting along the shores, where they had set up a large temporary camp.

The Captain returned on July 9th to Plymouth, where the Governor gave him a commission to a new campaign. He marched on that very night for the woods and pursuit of the enemy.

On July 11th he captured a large group of Indians in Middleboro; and on the same day, an engagement took place at Taunton.

During the period from July 12th to the 23rd, the English were engaged in a battle with the Indians at Monponsett, near the present town of Halifax, Massachusetts.

Within the days from July 17th to the 22nd, Captain Church's group were assigned to guide and guard some carts which were making their way to Taunton. It was during this period that he met up with and captured a group of Indians as he went through Assawompsett Neck, Acushnet, Apponnagansett, Mattapoisett, and the Sippican areas.

On July 30th, a post from Bridgewater announced that an army of Indians were threatening to cross the Titicut River (Taunton River) and enter the town. On this same afternoon Church and his men arrived at Monponsett (Halifax, Mass.). On July 31st the brisk Bridgewater troops attacked the Indians. Captain Church, who was heading toward the town, heard the fighting but did not then join in the pursuit.

It was on August 1, 1676, that, Church pursued the enemy and met up with them and spied King Philip as he was attempting to cross the Taunton River over a felled tree. Thereupon, Church and his men gave immediate chase, but Philip eluded the English once again. Nevertheless, Church took many surprised followers of the Wampanoag Sachem, including Philip's wife and his child.

During the next day Church scouted deeper into the swamps surrounding Rehoboth; and on August the 3rd he entered Bridgewater with his prisoners.

He arrived at Plymouth on August 4, 1676 with all his captives.

From August the 7th to the 9th, Church led an expedition into the locality of Dartmouth and captured a notorious Indian villain called by the name of Sam Barrow.

We find Captain Church on August 11th, leading another group of men into Pocasset where he went over on the ferry to see his wife at Major Sanford's. No sooner did he get there but he received intelligence that King Philip was at Mount Hope. Church returned to his men, and hastened to an immediate attack upon Mount Hope.

On August 12, 1676, Captain Church's command surprised Philip and lost no time in surrounding the Indian leader at the foot of the hill. Just as King Philip was fleeing down a little knoll, he was killed and fell on the southwest side of the hill at the foot of Mount Hope. Philip was on an upland Island in the midst of the swamp, and, of course, when he was alarmed he decided to run and make his escape through the swamp. The Wampanoag Sachem was killed by a bullet fired by a Saghonate Indian under Church's command named John Alderman.

A very short distance from the roadway that winds along the base of Mount Hope, there is an engraved stone marker at the spot where King Philip was killed.

An interesting account of this event, as dictated by Col. Church to his son in later years, written in Benjamin Church's own words and style, follows:

"Captain Church knowing it was Philip's custom to be foremost in the fight, went down to the Swamp and gave Capt. Williams of Situate the command of the right wing of the ambush, and placed an english-man and an Indian together behind such shelters of trees, etc., that he could find, and took care to place them at such distance as none might pass undis-covered between them, charged 'em to be careful of themselves, and of hurting their friends; And to fire at any that should come silently thro' the swamp: But it being somewhat further thro' the swamp than he was aware of, he wanted men to make up his am-buscade; having placed what men he had, he took Major Sanford by the hand, said, Sir, I have so placed them that tis scarce possible Philip should escape them. The same moment a shot whistled over their heads, and then the noise of a gun towards Philip's camp. Capt. Church at first tho't it might be some gun fired by accident: but before he could speak, a whole volley followed, which was earlier than he expected . . . the whole company that were with him fired upon the enemies shelter, before the indians had time to rise from their sleep, and so overshot them. But their shelter was open on that side next the swamp, built so on purpose for the convenience of flight on occasion. They were soon in the swamp and Philip the foremost, who starting at the first gun threw his Petunk (pocket apron) and powder horn over his head, catc'd up his gun, and ran as fast as he could scamper, without any more clothes than his small breeches and stockings, and ran directly upon two of Capt. Churches ambush; they let him come fair with shot, and the English man's gun missing fire, he bid the Indian fire away, and he so to purpose, sent one musket bullet thro' his heart, and another not above two inches from it; he fell upon his face in the mud and water with his gun under him. By this time the enemy perceived they were way-laid on the east side of the swamp, tack'd short about. One of the enemy who seem'd to be a great surly old fellow, Hollow'd with a loud voice, & ofter called out Iootash, Iootash (this word actually means, Fight, but was used by the Indians to be, Stand Firm. Stand Firm) Capt. Church called to his indian Peter (Awashonk's Son) and ask'd who that was that called so? He answered that it was old Annawon, Philip's great Captain, calling on his soldiers to stand to it and fight stoutly . . . The man that shot Philip ran with all speed to Capt. Church, and informed him of his exploit, who commanded him to be silent about it, & let no man more know it, until they had drove the swamp clean . . . and when Captain Church gave them the news of Philip's death; upon which the whole army gave three loud Hussa's . . . Capt. Church ordered his body to be pulled out of the mire on to the upland, so some of Capt. Church's indians took hold of him by his stockings, and some by his small breeches, (being outherwise naked) and drew him thro' the Mud unto the Upland, and a doleful, great, naked, dirty beast, he looked like. Capt. Church then said, that foasmuch as he had caused many and englishmans body to lye unburied and rot above the ground, that not one of his bones should be buried. And calling his indian Executioner, bid him behead and quarter him. Accordingly, he came with his Hatchet and stood over him, but before he struck he made a small Speech directing it to Philip; and said, He had been a very great Man, and had made many a man afraid of him, but so big as he was he would now chop his . . . for him; and so went to work, and did as he was ordered. Philip having one very remarkable hand being much scarr'd, occassioned by the splitting of a Pistol in it formerly. Capt. Church gave the head and that hand to Alderman, the Indian who shot him, to show to such Gentlemen as would bestow gratuities upon him; and accordingly he got many a peny by it. This being on the last day of the Week, the Captain with his company returned to the Island, tarryed there until Tuesday; and then went off and ranged thro' all the Woods to Plymouth, and received their Premium, which was Thirty Shillings per head, for the Enemies which they had killed or taken, instead of all Wages; and Philips head went as the same price."

And so ends Captain Church's own recording of the Death of King Philip . . .

The head of King Philip was later put on display atop a pole for twenty-four years at Plymouth. His hand (or hands) were sent to the Government at Boston as a souvenir from the people of Plymouth.

The Captain later went back to Rhode Island with his soldiers in pursuit of Anawon, Philip's Chief Captain. This story we will touch upon during a sketch of Anawon.

It was also said that among those who were killed with Philip on the very same day, was the Indian who had fired the first musket at the beginning of the war. Of the thousands of warriors claimed by the Narragansett tribes only one hundred remained.

The Wampanoags as a Federation were no more.

The cost of the war to the Colonies was estimated at half a million dollars. Six hundred men were killed and thirteen towns were completely burned. The homes of six hundred families were ruined.

It must be said of Philip's character that he remained true to his people, fighting to the last for what he believed was right. Indeed, his was a gallant attempt by a great leader to preserve the heritage he was born into.

The clash of the cultures was inevitable: . . . and this direct quote spoken by King Philip to his friend, John Borden of Rhode Island, eloquently sums up the Indian's attitude at the time: *"The English who came first to this country were but an handful of people, forlorn, poor and distressed. My father was then sachem, he relieved their distresses in the most kind and hospitable manner. He gave them land to plant and build upon ....... they flourished and increased. By various means they got possessed of a great part of his territory. But he still remained their friend till he died. My elder brother became sachem ....... He was seized and confined and thereby thrown into illness and died. Soon after I became sachem they disarmed all my people . . . their land was taken . . . But a small part of the dominion of my ancestors remains. I am determined not to live until I have no country."*

With Philip's death, the war, in so far as the Plymouth Colony was concerned, came practically to an end. The remaining few Indians and others of the Wampanoags who had escaped death and continued under the leadership of Anawon, Philip's Chief Captain, were captured by Captain Benjamin Church and his troops August 28, 1676 in a section of Rehoboth, Massachusetts at a location now called, "Anawon's Rock" that is located on the main road from Providence to Taunton, (Route 44.) We will have more to say of Anawon later.

On September 5, 1676, the venerable Indian Fighter, Captain Church marched with his men into that section of the country now known as Rochester, Massachusetts and took as prisoners the people of the chief of the Assawompsett Tribe.

Captain Church learned that their Chief, Tuspaquin, "The Black Sachem," who was married to Mionie, Massasoit's daughter, was away at the time in the vicinity of Agawam, now Rochester, Massachusetts, which included then the site of the present section of Wareham, Massachusetts. Church left two old squaws there to inform the chief at his return that he had taken the Indian prisoners to Plymouth and that he intended to spare their lives and that of the chief, if Tuspaquin would go of his own will to Plymouth along with any others that might be with him.

The "Black Sachem" did comply with this word, but we found that he was put to death at Plymouth some time in September of that same year.

From the facts handed down in the various early recordings that formed the material for this sketch of King Philip, we have learned that Philip was without question the commander of all the Indian warriors who took part in the war against the Colonies.

For the record, it now would be proper to list the names of those Panseis (warrior leaders) from the Wampanoag Federation who were directly under Philip in the campaigns: Anawon, Cawnacome, Obbatinnua, Nattawahunt, Corbitant, Chuckatabak, Quadequina, Hutmoiden, Apanno (Epanow), Tuspaquin and Akkompoin. Those from other Indian Federations included; Pumham, a chief of one of the Narragansett Tribes and rated by some writers as second to Philip among the Indian leaders; another captain serving under Philip was Quinapen who was a nephew to Miantonomo, Chief of the Narragansett Federation; and later, Miantonomo's son, Canochet took over the Sachemship upon his father's death. We do know that Weetammo, Squaw Sachem of the Pocassets, though a woman, proved one of the pivots in nearly all phases of the war.

Since the year 1917, the R. F. Haffenreffer family have owned the lands that include historic Mount Hope. The United States Military now have an important defense installation within the area, but visitors to Mount Hope can still gain access to an elevated rock formation believed to have been used by King Philip as a throne of state during many of his Indian councils. This granite chair is located directly to the north and at the base of the hill, facing easterly looking across the magnificent view over Mount Hope Bay. Located just north of Mount Hope summit and beyond King Philip's throne is the museum that houses the Haffenreffer Collection of Indian relics and artifacts, now open to the public through the courtesy of Brown University of Providence, Rhode Island.

# Chapter VIII

## TRIBUTE TRIBES

## of

## The Wampanoag Indian Federation

*Site of this grave is on Bonehill Road at Cumaquid in Barnstable, Massachusetts.*

*Photo by Author*

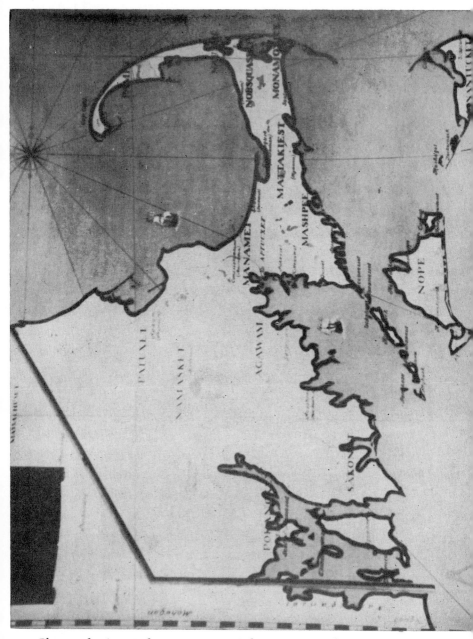

*Photograph of original map, property of the Aptucxet Trading Post, Bourne Historical Society, Bourne, Massachusetts.   Courtesy of Mrs. George Hiltwein.*

*Photo by Author.*

# THE WAMPANOAG INDIAN FEDERATION

In attempting a work of this nature one meets a bulwark of contradictory matter as set down in the hidden paragraphs of early records. When trying to list the separate tribes that made up the Wampanoag Federation, one encounters a task that assumes proportions that make it nearly impossible to accomplish. It is the researcher's task however, to sift and evaluate these notations, and one readily sees reason for so great and problematical a variance in purported interpretations of the facts.

It is known that the Wampanoag Indian had no real permanent homesite. He moved from place to place as the whim and need of the moment motivated him to do so. Wherever he did move, we found that he usually designated the area with a descriptive name. The net result was the early writer's notation of those sections which appeared to him as tribes. This made an accumulation of names and places that far exceeded expectation and tended to confuse some facts, adding many place names and descriptive titles as tribes when actually they were not.

In the following chapters, we will list only those whose histories have shown them as substantial residences, or villages, or tribes; but we do ask the reader's pardon if occasional subsidiary sites creep into the text.

## THE AGAWAM - WAMPANOAG TRIBE

Agawam was the Indian name of the settlement near the Agawam river. This village was located in a section of so-called "Great Bear Swamp," located about a mile and a half southwest of the village of Rochester, Massachusetts and a short distance east of a road that led to Mattapoisett, Massachusetts.

Some have said that it was in what is now Wareham, Massachusetts. The name comes from the Wampanoag word meaning, "low land close by a river"; hence, that section of Wareham along the river close by the narrows.

The tribal leader known during the period of King Philip's war was called by name of Sanballet, alias Sam Barrow, whom Benjamin Church described as a "noted a rougue as any among the enemy." His name appears on the Old Colony records in a list of the parties who destroyed Clark's Garrison.

Sam Barrow was captured during one of Captain Church's expeditions between the 7th and 9th of August 1676. His captor had this to say about the event, "Because of his inhuman murders and barbarities, the court had allowed him no quarter but was to be forthwith put to death, and therefore he was to prepare for it. Barrow replied, 'that the sentence against him was just, and that indeed he was a-shamed to live any longer and desired no more favor than to smoke a whiff of tobacco before his execution.' When he had taken a few whiffs he said, 'He was ready'; upon which one of Captain Church's Indians sunk his hatchet into his brain."

Sam Barrow's son, Tatoson, alias Tautozen, was one of the two companions who fled with Tuspaquin, as mentioned during Church's capture of a band of Indians on September 5, 1676 during the final stages of the war.

At the time of Sam Barrow's capture and death, Tatoson and his own little boy of about 8 years old made their escape, along with one old squaw, into the section of his own country of Agawam.

We recall from the last chapter that Church had left word with two squaws advising them to tell their Chief Tuspaquin and his two other companions to give themselves up upon their return. Tatoson was one of those followers who later surrendered at Plymouth. The old squaw who was with the child later appeared at Sandwich and told the authorities that Tatoson's child had fallen sick during the flight and died. She told them that she buried him in the woods and offered to take the officials to his grave, but she never had the opportunity to do this for it is said that she immediately fell ill and died suddenly.

## THE NAUSETT - WAMPANOAG TRIBE

The old historian's account of the event that took place on the beach of Nausett in Cape Cod, in the locality of what is now Eastham, Massachusetts, and described by them as the "First Encounter" introduces us to another Wampanoag Tribute Tribe called the Nausetts.

It was just three days before the landing of the Pilgrims at Plymouth that this event occurred. A small scouting party had left the Mayflower in their shallop and while encamped overnight on the beach, they were suddenly awakened at about five o'clock in the morning by the sound of unfamiliar screams, best described by this quaint phonetic spelling handed down by the early writer, "Woatch, — Woach — Ha-Ha — Hoah — Woach." Concomitantly, the air was filled with arrows that fell in the midst of the explorers. Again we quote from the old historian,

"Our men were no sooner come to their arms but the enemy was ready to assault them. There was a lustie man and no wit less valiant who was thought to be their captain, stood behind a tree within half a musket shot of us and there let his arrow fly at us . . . he stood three shots of a musket. At length one took as he said full aim at him, he gave an extraordinary cry, and away they all went."

While the white men were curiously examining the arrows that had fallen, a dog appeared at the Indian's ambush spot and began barking at the English. Within an instant, an Indian appeared again, whistled after his pet and together they ran into the forest.

The Indians who participated in this brief skirmish were members of the Nausett Tribe under the Chief called by the name of Aspinet, who was a sagamore of the Wampanoag Federation acknowledging allegiance to Massasoit.

The exact spot of this encounter is said to have been called by the Indians as "Nemskeket," situated in the present town of Eastham, Massachusetts; which was incorporated June 2, 1646, and which at that time included the present sites of Orleans and Wellfleet. Orleans was set off from Eastham on March 3, 1797, and Wellfleet on June 16, 1763. Wellfleet was then called by the Indian, Punonakauit.

It was three days after this so called "First Encounter," that the English landed at the site of Plymouth, which was then called Patuxet by the Indians, and which was, prior to the plague, site of the Patuxet Indian village.

Another interesting tale that has been handed down to us involving the Nausetts and their Chief Aspinet came about as a result of a boy's wandering and his getting lost. The Pilgrim boy's name was John Billington. He got lost in the woods about six months after the Pilgrims landed at Plymouth.

Upon finding the boy missing the Settlers appealed to Massasoit. It was not long after that the people at Plymouth beheld the sight of a large group of Indians approaching their village carrying on their shoulders in great triumph the missing lad. He was adorned with Indian beads and seemed none the worse for his experience. He was returned to his parents amidst great clamorings befitting what must have been to the Indians an auspicious occasion. As a reward, Chief Aspinet and the Chief Iyanough, who had found the boy, were each presented with an English made knife, a gift tremendously esteemed by them. The boy later said that the Indians treated him with as much tenderness and courtesy as he had ever encountered.

In the year 1622, having previously secured permission from Massasoit to carry on trade with the local tribes, the Pilgrims embarked on a trip into the Nausett country. As a result of an unusually tempestuous storm that drove their shallop on to shore at a point where they had not intended to land, and due to the sudden illness of their Indian guide, Squanto, (who later died as a result of this attack), — the expedition was brought into contact with a few Indians from other villages.

## THE MANAMOYK - WAMPANOAG TRIBE

An account handed down to us from the records of Winslow, states; "But here at a place called Manamoyk, (now Monomoy in Chatham, Massachusetts). Though they had determined to make a second assay, yet God had otherwise disposed, who struck Tisquantum (Squanto) with sickness, in as so much that he there died, which crossed their southward trading, and the more because the Master's sufficiency was doubted, and the season very tempestrous and not fit to go upon discovery, having no guide to direct them."

This trip that came so near to failure owing to the death of Squanto was not abandoned, for he, just before his death, managed to introduce his English friends to the Chief of Manamoyk and his people, who received the English very enthusiastically and offered them stores of venison and other food which they seemed to have in abundance. These Indians sold them eight hogshead of corn and beans.

The Chief of Manamoyk at that time was believed to be Mattaquason. In the year 1665, his son John Quason Taswott had succeeded him as leader of the Manamoyks.

## THE MATTAKEESET - WAMPANOAG TRIBE

While still on this trading expedition, the settlers visited a village called Mattakeeset. Here they met a sub-chief of the village by the name of Keencomsett who also entertained them in a friendly manner. They purchased ten hogsheads of corn from him.

Once again while sailing the waters near the Nau-sett country, another storm suddenly broke and forced their shallop on shore, damaging it to the extent where they could not readily get the corn on board. Chief Aspinet graciously allowed them to store their purchases in his custody until the English were able to return for it.

The governor returned home by land and was particularly pleased with the way he was treated by the Indians along the route.

Nevertheless; in spite of all this show of pleasure and courtesy by Aspinet, we know that he was one of the Indian leaders in the conspiracy with the Massachusetts Indians who planned to overthrow the Plymouth settlement. This plot was disclosed to the Governor by Massasoit when he charged Hobba-mock to tell Winslow of it during the latter's attend-ance at Massasoit's illness. As a result of this dis-closure, Aspinet was routed, along with several of his people and other conspirators. He fled into the swamp lands and was never heard of again. It is be-lieved that he died as a result of these circumstances.

Through accounts of further trips made by the Settlers into the Cape Cod area we find mention of these other tribute tribes of the Wampanoag Fed-eration; Punonakauit, now Wellfleet; Namskaket; situated by the creek of the same name. The village of Mattakeeset is now Yarmouth, Mass., but it then included a portion of what is now Barnstable, Mass.

## IYANOUGH

The Chief of the Mattakeeset country was called Iyanough. He was a sagamore of the Wampanoag Federation.

It was in June of 1621 that the English first met him and described him as, "a man personable, gentle, courteous, and fair conditioned about 26 years old, indeed not a savage, save in attire". They also met an old Indian squaw here whom they believed to be well over 100 years old.

We have noted that it was this Chief who aided in the return of the lost Billington boy. The records of the early History of Barnstable, Massachusetts cite Iyanough particularly for his kindnesses to the Pilgrims.

From a news release issued by "Tales of Cape Cod, Inc.," of Hyannis, Massachusetts and dated April 7, 1957, we take the following: "Many kindnesses have been recorded from Iyanough to the white man, which makes his death a tragic contrast. Escaping from the white men who were in uprising against the Indians, having been warned of a reverse conspiracy in the making, Iyanough contracted a disease from hiding in the swamps and died from its effects. Iyanough's domain lay along the north side of Barnstable, but tradition also has him owning lands on the site of Hyannis Port."

In the year 1861, Iyanough's grave was believed to have been uncovered in a field at Cummaquid. The bones and relics now repose in the museum at Plymouth, Mass.

The spot at the site of the empty grave has been marked with a tablet placed there in 1894 by the Cape Cod Historical Society, and bears the following inscription:

*On this spot was buried the*
*Sachem Iyanough*
*The friend and entertainer*
*of the Pilgrims, July 1621\**
*Erected by the Cape Cod Historical Society*

Tales of Cape Cod, Inc. recently acquired the site of Iyanough's grave. The society hopes to re-possess this venerable Indian's bones and replace them within the grave.

It is interesting to note here that records show that Hyannis, Wianno and other places on Cape Cod, Massachusetts are named in honor of this Sagamore of the Wampanoag Federation. Many corruptions of his name have been handed down, among which, are; Iyannos, Hyanos, Jannos, Yannis, Highannus and Hyanus.

## THE QUISSET-WAMPANOAG TRIBE

The Quissets, sometimes listed as Cooxisset, were located in the vicinity of Wood's Hole and Falmouth, Massachusetts.

Some of the other lesser Tribute Tribes of the Wampanoag Indian Federation mentioned only by name in various early records included the following:

Assameekg, Cowsumpsit, Coquasquscit,
Miacomit, Nashamoiess, Nashanekammuck,
Ohkonekemme, Pachade, Quittaub,
Sancheacantacket, Shimoah, Talhanio,
Toikiming and Wacchimuqut.

---

\* This date should be 1623. The grave marker carries the wrong date.

## THE PATUXET-WAMPANOAG TRIBE

All we know of the Patuxet Tribe comes from the fact that it was mentioned as having been located at the site of Plymouth town.

The famous Wampanoag Indian, Squanto, claimed that he was the sole survivor of the Patuxet people. If it were not for these facts we might never have learned of the existence of Patuxet as one of the Wampanoag Tribute Tribes.

Now that we have mentioned the Patuxet Tribe, we return to our sequence, and go into a brief biography of the only well-known member of that tribe; the Indian known to the English as Squanto.

*Massasoit's profile rock, a natural formation, located within the Freetown State Forest in Assonet, Massachusetts.*                    *Photo by Author*

# Chapter IX

# SQUANTO and HOBBAMOCK

## Saviors of the Settlers

*Replicas of the first Pilgrim homes. Located in Plymouth, Massachusetts.*

*Photo by Author*

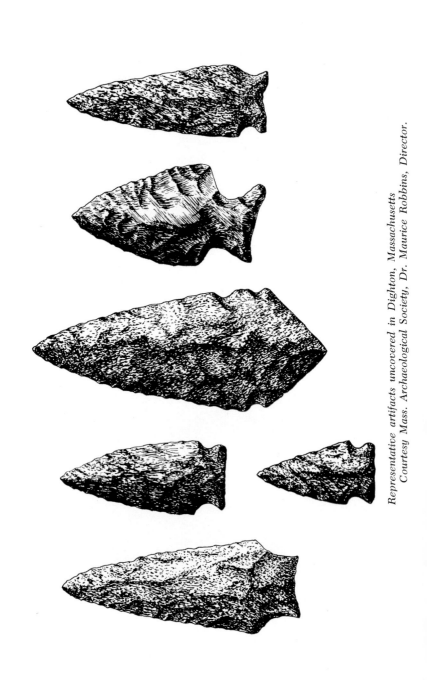

*Representative artifacts uncovered in Dighton, Massachusetts*
*Courtesy Mass. Archaeological Society, Dr. Maurice Robbins, Director.*

# SQUANTO

Samoset was the first Indian to make an appearance before the English. He was the Indian who walked boldly into Plymouth and called out the famous salutation, "Welcome Englishmen!" Samoset told the English that he was not of any local tribe but was a Sagamore of the tribes then located in the area now the State of Maine. He said that he had learned to speak English from the frequent visits of white fishermen to the coasts of his country.

He is the Indian who first told them that their settlement was on the spot that the Indians once called Patuxet. He also revealed that a few years before, this tribe along with several others, was swept away by the ravages of the plague, "until in the whole Pokanoket country there were but five hundred Wampanoags remaining alive."

It was not until his third visit, on March 22, 1621, that he brought along and introduced to the Pilgrims the Indian called Squanto. As was the Indian custom, this Indian appears to have been called at various times, Tisquantum, Squantum, and Squanto. History records his name as, Squanto.

Squanto spoke a better English than his friend, Samoset, and he, himself, confirmed the fact that he was one of the several Indians who was kidnapped by Captain Thomas Hunt and sold into slavery in the year 1614. Upon his release he was taken to London where he lived with a man by the name of Slainie, who was very kind to him. In the year 1619, Squanto returned to his native country with a Captain Thomas Dermer (a story we related to the reader in an earlier chapter). Squanto was the Indian interpretor during Captain Dermer's excursion into the Pokanoket Country just prior to the coming of the Pilgrims.

He told the settlers that he was the sole survivor of his tribe, the Patuxets, having found it so upon his return home.

Squanto carved for himself a prominent place in the history of the early settlement of New England as he became the valuable assistant, guide, and "Tongue" of the early settlers, whom he served from the time of his appearance until his death two years later.

It was Squanto who taught the English how to plant and cultivate their corn and catch the fish called, "alewives" that to this very day swim up the streams in great schools in the early spring just at planting time. He showed the English how to fertilize their gardens by placing a fish along side the seeded hills. He guided them throughout the forest in their quest for game and trade. It was said that he adopted their religion, and upon his death requested that his belongings be distributed among his white friends as a reminder of his love for them.

Nevertheless; as later events proved, Squanto became a rather ambitious and jealous sort and, it seems, had his sights aimed at some lofty rank in the Wampanoag government. He died long before he could realize this ambition. Thereby, history remembers him as the valuable assistant to the Settlers; a good friend, interpreter and guide of the Pilgrims.

We know that he acted as guide on many of their expeditions and explorations. On September 28,

1621, he was the Englishmen's guide when a group of them left under the leadership of Miles Standish on a trip to Boston Harbor, then known as Massachusetts Bay; "to discover and view that bay and trade with ye natives . . . partly to see the country, partly to make peace with them, and partly to procure their trucke, or barter."

This particular voyage commenced just before midnight but it was late in the day when they arrived at the bay on the site now known as "Squantum's Point", where a Cairn was placed in later years to commemorate the landing of the group on that spot. The date on the tablet states their arrival as September 30, 1621.

We quote Mr. Bradford's account of this trip; "They returned in safety, and brought home a good quantity of beaver, and made report of ye place, wishing that they had been there seated; but it seems ye Lord who assigns to all men ye bounds of their habitation, had appointed it for another use . . . and they found kind entertainment there."

We have mentioned the case of the lost boy, John Billington, and in reference to this event, an Indian by the name of Hobbamock appeared before the Colonists as a special envoy from Massasoit to help facilitate the boy's return. This particular Indian held a high position in the Great Sachem's council, and by virtue of being one of the keenest warriors of the Wampanoag tribes; he was termed a Panseis and Sagamore of the Federation.

Both Squanto and Hobbamock remained at Plymouth until their deaths, and during their lives were quite valuable, and, with Massasoit, have been termed saviors to the Colonists during their early struggles for survival in the new world.

During the month of August in the year 1621, while Hobbamock and Squanto were visiting friends at Nemasket they were attacked by Chief Corbitant, sagamore of the Mettapoiset and Pocasset Tribes. Hobbamock managed to escape, and having last seen Squanto struggling for his life at the hands of Corbitant, he ran fifteen miles to Plymouth where he rallied Miles Standish and his army, who speedily set out for Nemasket to, "rescue him if he were alive or to punish Corbitant if he had been killed."

Upon arriving at Nemasket, the English learned that Squanto was alive and had been threatened only. His assailant had run away into the woods toward his own county at Mettapoiset, now Gardiner's Neck near Swansea, Massachusetts. Corbitant later appeared before the English at Plymouth in September, 1621, to make amends for his conduct.

A few months after this episode, Hobbamock confided to the settlers that he had heard rumors that the Massachusetts and Narragansett Federations were endeavoring to secure the Wampanoag's assistance in plotting against the English. He cautioned the Settlers that since they were leaving for proposed exploration, the Indians intended to take advantage of Miles Standish's absence and strike at the settlers. He added that he had received word that proved Squanto was in sympathy with the plotters. As a result of this information, the Governor decided to send both Squanto and Hobbamock along on board the shallop. Hardly had the group set sail, than an Indian messenger appeared on the scene bringing news that confirmed Hobbamock's intelligence, and the boat was recalled. This messenger added that the story was not rumor but fact and it was believed that all of Massasoit's people were indeed to participate.

Hobbamock vehemently objected to this intelligence, saying that he was sure that his Sachem would cause no such action without first consulting his council, of which he, Hobbamock, was a Panseis and Sagamore. As proof of his contention, Hobbamock dispatched his wife to Sowams country, where she privately learned that all was quiet, and there was no conspiracy of the sort.

Massasoit finally received word of this rumor of conspiracy and was so greatly shocked that he personally appeared at Plymouth to clear himself of all the false rumored charges. Learning that Squanto had assisted in spreading the rumor, Massasoit requested Governor Bradford to forfeit the Indian to the Sachem's jurisdiction. This was denied by the Governor, because the Englishman knew that, according to Indian law, Squanto would be immediately killed as a traitor.

When Squanto was formally accused of participation in spreading this rumor of conspiracy, he offered no denial and placed himself at the mercy of the Governor; and he, in turn, having a "friend in court," was spared punishment. After many repeated entreaties made by Massasoit to the Governor asking for Squanto's custody, the demands were later dropped.

In regard to Squanto's ambitious qualities we quote the following taken from a record of the times; "They (the English) began to see that Tisquantum sought his own end and played his own game. By putting the Indians in fear, and drawing gifts from them to enrich himself; making them believe he could stir up war against whom he would and make peace for them he would. Yea, he made them believe they kept the plague buried in the ground and could send it amongst whom they (English) would, which did much terrify the Indians, and made them depend more on him, and seek more to him than to Massasoit; which procured him envy, and like to have cost him his life. For after the discovery of his practices, Massasoit sought it both privately and openly; which caused him to stick close to the English and never durst go from them till he died."

It is said that during the time he was with the English, after they learned of his ambitions, they took advantage of his jealousy toward Hobbamock and, in order to gain better services from both, they played one against the other. "The Governor seeming to countenance one and Standish the other."

Squanto died suddenly in 1622 of a fever, "attended with bleeding much at the nose." Before his death he made the requests mentioned before; and added that he wished the Governor would pray for him directing his prayers to the white man's God, and that he preferred being buried in the Pilgrim's cemetery.

We know that Hobbamock remained a faithful servant to the English until his death, the date of which is unknown. Factually, he proved himself a more valuable aid to the English, due, no doubt, to his high position within the Federation. Wherever he went he was recognized by all the Indians as one of the great panseis of Massasoit. This, of course, influenced them to a greater degree in dealing with the Pilgrims, and was much to the advantage of the English.

## THE ASSONET - WAMPANOAG TRIBE

Very little of interest has been recorded about the Assonet Tribe. These people inhabited the area now called Freetown and Assonet, Massachusetts. During the sachemship of Wamsutta, their leader was called Tabadacason.

It was said that after Massasoit's death, there appeared in the forest of the Assonets a rock formation so much in the image of the great Sachem that the aboriginies came for miles to gaze in wonder at it.

According to the old Wampanoag custom of not mentioning the names of deceased leaders, this stone face was never openly acknowledged as the profile of their dead Sachem.

This natural rock formation has been preserved to this day, and is located a few feet off the main highway in the Freetown State Forest near Assonet, Massachusetts and is easily accessible on foot. It is now called, "Profile Rock."

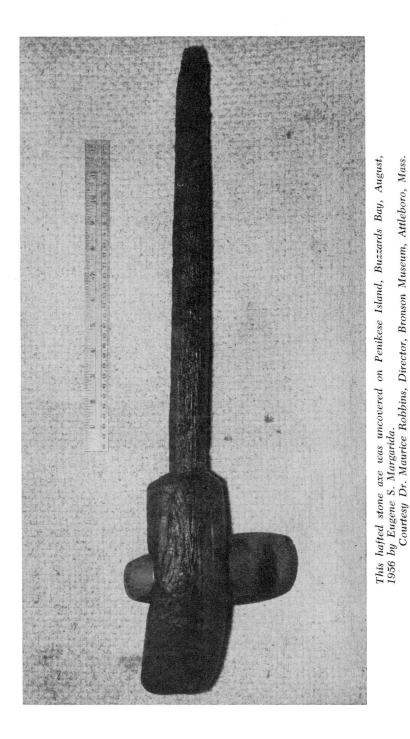

This hafted stone axe was uncovered on Penikese Island, Buzzards Bay, August, 1956 by Eugene S. Margarida.

Courtesy Dr. Maurice Robbins, Director, Bronson Museum, Attleboro, Mass.

# Chapter X

## TUSPAQUIN

### "The Black Sachem"
### Chief of the Assawompsett Tribe

*While field workers of the Massachusetts Archaeological Society watch, Dr. Maurice Robbins, painstakingly uncovers a "find" at the excavating site in the Assawompsett country.*

Courtesy Mass. Archaeological Society

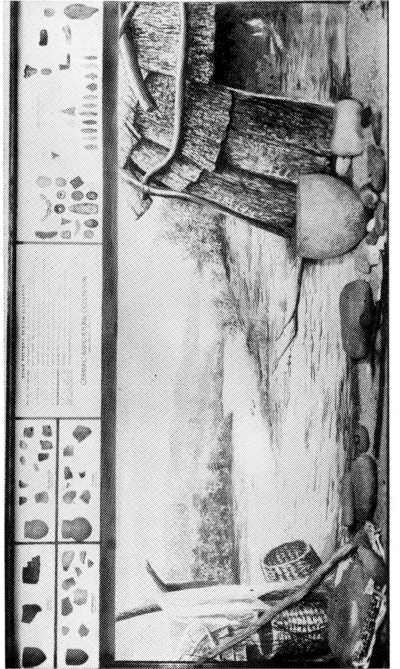

*Photograph of Diorama at Bronson Museum in Attleboro, Mass. showing agricultural implements, pottery and basketry outside typical Wampanoag dwelling.*

*Courtesy Mass. Archaeological Society, Dr. Maurice Robbins, Director.*

# THE ASSAWOMPSETT - WAMPANOAG TRIBE

The Assawompsett Tribe inhabited the section of the Pokanoket country lying within the area now including the Town of Lakeville, Massachusetts and Middleboro, Massachusetts and parts of Freetown, Rochester and Acushnet, Massachusetts, in the vicinity of Assawompsett and Long Ponds.

As the reader knows, the Chief of this tribe was called, Tuspaquin; alias Watuspaquin, "The Black Sachem of the Assawompsetts." He, too, was a sagamore of the Wampanoag Federation. His residence was in that section of his country known as Assawompsett Neck, the section of land that lies between Assawompsett Pond and Long Pond.

It is known that he was a powerful Sagamore carrying authority over several of the other neighboring Indian villages.

We know that Tuspaquin was married to Mionie, Massasoit's daughter.

From the historian, Drake, we learn that in 1676 the Assawompsett Tribe had 300 warriors who figured quite prominently in King Philip's war. It is believed that Indians under Tuspaquin, dealt the savage assault on Scituate on April 20, 1676.

The Sachem's son, William Tuspaquin, whose Indian name was Mantowapuct, was known as the chief of the Nemasket Tribe whose village was at what is called the Four Corners of Middleboro, Massachusetts, and also parts of that town that lie close to Taunton; hence the close relationship between those tribes. Mantowapuct died quite early in the war as we find no further mention of him after the first few months of the year 1675.

In a previous chapter we touched upon the facts that led to Tuspaquin's surrender at the closing stages of the war in the year 1676 and of his death shortly afterward.

Bearing in mind the fact that Benjamin Church had given his word that the Black Sachem's life would be spared if he voluntarily surrendered to the people at Plymouth, it is said that the Sachem submitted himself with the hope that he was to be made a captain under the illustrious and well-liked Captain Church. It is recorded that, upon his surrender, the authorities at Plymouth declared that, "the promise of a captain's place depended upon his being impenetrable by bullets, a claim that the Indians had made of him." Taking advantage of Captain Church's absence, the Colonists subjected Tuspaquin to this test before a firing squad, with the expected result of his death. Here we let the reader draw his own conclusion, but we have in mind the prevailing English belief in supernatural manifestations in those early years.

Several years later we find that a tribe called by the English name of, "Betty's Neck Tribe," occupied a village located in the area that once was Tuspaquin's residence; that is, in the Assawompsett Neck.

Still others of the Wampanoag tribute tribes of which we find very little mention, are:

THE COAXET TRIBE
THE APPONAGANSETT TRIBE
THE ACOOSHNET TRIBE
THE SCONTICUT TRIBE

These small Indian villages all occupied the territory of ancient Dartmouth. The Sagamore of these tribes, in King Philip's time, was called Monyocam. The Acooshnets (Acushnet) occupied the territory that later became New Bedford, Massachusetts. The Apponagansetts inhabited the area now known as Dartmouth, Massachusetts. The Sconticuts roamed the territory now designated as Fairhaven, Massachusetts, and the Coaxets resided in the sections now known as Acoaxet and Westport, Massachusetts, particularly those parts now South Westport, Head of Westport (called then by the Indians, Paquachuck, and meaning, "the clear view hill") along both sides of the Westport River, and that part of the country now known as Horseneck.

At this point it might be interesting to note another example of the easy corruption of Indian words. We take, for instance, the last mentioned section, "Horseneck" - - - this being a corruption of the Indian word, "Hassaneghk; — which was the Indian descriptive word applied to a white settler's dwelling situated in the locality. This dwelling consisted of four stoned walls with a pitched roof, and the only word in the Wampanoag language that best described it was, Hassaneghk. Thereby, it is easy to see how through the years, the white man in imitating the phonetic Indian sounds for the word, finally corrupted it into the present Horseneck.

In a paper written by Captain Thomas R. Rodman and printed in Volume 3 of "The Old Dartmouth Historical Sketches", dated December 29, 1903; the Captain mentions these Dartmouth Indians and incidents of their times as; "Of incidents in the history of Dartmouth during the King Philip war, I know nothing, beyond that narrated, until July 20, 1676 or some date thereabouts, when Captain Church was ordered to guard a train of carts to the army of Major

Bradford, stationed at Taunton, he delivered his train, and then hearing of the celebrated Tishpa-quine, at Assawompsett, now Middleboro, started with a force of English and Indians to attack him.

"He had proposed to encamp at Assawampsett and Long Ponds, attacks the enemy, driving them into the swamp. He then marches a mile farther, halts until midnight, when he resumes his march to the south, probably following the trail which, I judge now to have developed into Long Plain Road, toward Cushnet, where all the houses were burnt. He crosses the river by the ford at head of tide water, where the Acushnet Bridge now stands, and, moving west, camps on the higher land, which is between the Acushnet Valley and the great cedar swamp. Having set a watch at the crossing, he takes his company into a thicket for sleep.

"The next morning (21st) he sees Indians viewing their tracks, leading up from the crossing, and send-ing out scouts, captures with his family, "Little Eyes" — a hostile from the Squaw-Sachem Awashonk's friendly band. Captain Church then leads his army along the river on the west side. Finding an old canoe, he sends "Little Eyes" and his band to an island, probably Palmer's Island, under the charge of his cousin, Captain Lightfoot, and proceeds with his company across the neck of Clark's Point, passing over the ground now occupied by the Potomska and other mills, and thence along the head of Clark's Cove, and up the hill, till, following the trail or road to the head of the Apponagansett River, he comes to the neighborhood of Russell's orchards, or Rus-sell's Garrison. There they 'clap'd into a thicket, and there lod'g the rest of the night without any fire.'"

Captain Thomas R. Rodman went on and wrote "In the morning, drawing nearer to the orchard they discover 'some of the enemy, who had been there the day before, and had beat down all the apples and carried them away': they discovered also where they had lodged that night, and saw the ground where they set their baskets bloody . . . with the flesh of swine, etc., which they had killed that day. The Indians who had lain under the fences without any fires, seemed by the marks they had left behind to be very numerous. The dew on the grass where brushed away, showed they had not been long gone, and Captain Church started at once in pursuit of them. 'Traveling three miles or more they came into the country road, where the track parted; one parcel steered toward the west end of the great Cedar swamp and the other to the east end.' I think their route may have been by either of the trails, which were to become respectively, the Slocum and Tucker Roads, and which led to the site of the village of Smith Mills. Here the ways part that on the east following that part of the old trail from Plymouth to Howland's Ferry, which we call today the Ezra Hathaway road; the other, on the west, leading by way of Faunces Corner, and thence to the firm ground near Braleys Station of today. Where the two trails diverge, the force divided, the Indians going west of the swamp and Captain Church with the English, east. The ruins of John Cook's house at Cushnet were appointed as a rendezvous, and this shows, first, that John Cook's house had been destroyed; second, that Cushnet was the designation of that locality. The ruined house was near the Fairhaven terminus of the Coggeshall Street Bridge. Church's party proceeding by the old Plymouth trail, comes to a miry swamp where they find Indians picking hurtleberries. This was probably on the line of Shawmut Avenue. He attacks them, kills three and takes 63 prisoners; is informed that there are many Indians in the Great Swamp, that Philip himself is only two miles away; that the party captured were left there by 100 Indians who had gone to Sconticut Neck to kill cattle and horses for food, and had crossed the river, Acushnet, at its head. Captain Church concluded that he must cross with his party lower down. He does not tell us where or how he crossed . . . Then, calling 'Lightfoot' from Palmer's Island, he goes with him and Mr. Delano, one of his company, to a meadow, whence they see the Indians pass on their return from Sconticut Neck, en route for the upper crossing. After the Indians had gone on, the main body, the prisoners and 'Lightfoot's' party . . . made all haste for Mattapoisett River."

Captain Rodman ends his paper with no other references made to matters pertaining to our Wampanoag Indians.

The word Acooshnet is the descriptive Indian term meaning, "at the place we get to the other side." Apponagansett, meant; "At the place where the little waters enter the big waters." Coaxet is believed to mean, "the place, or hill, near conquered land;" and this conquered land was, Sogkonate, for the word, "Sogkonate," — describes, "The third conquered territories." Evidently, The Wampanoags at some time had obtained the Sakonnet country through some Indian war with a neighboring tribe.

# Chapter XI

# AWASHONKS
## "The Squaw Sachem of the Sogkonates"

# Friend and Ally of the White Man

*The Awashonks Memorial Boulder in Wilbour Woods
at Little Compton, Rhode Island.*
            *Courtesy Howard C. Mandell*

# North

# PLAN OF WATUPPA INDIAN RESERVATION

# FALL RIVER, MASS.

3 acres and 59 rods in this angle.

| | | | | | | |
|---|---|---|---|---|---|---|
| 10 r. 7 f. | 10 r 10 f. | 10. 12 f. | 10 r 15 f. | 11 R. 3 ft ¼ | 11 R. 7 f. | 11 R. 10 f. ¼ |

This lott belong to Lydia a grand daughter of James Dumas.
No. 25. 6 a. 128 r.

This lott belong to Hannah Cooper daughter of Samuel Titicutt.
No. 23. 6. 124.

This lott belong to John Mary & Mercy, the children of John Schoonick.
No. 24. 6 a 128 r.

This lott belong to Comfort and Thankful grand children of Benjamin Squannamauy.
No. 21. 6 a. 128 r.

This lott belong to Daniel & James, children of Sarah Quan.
No. 21.—6 a. 128 r.

This lott belong to Mercy & Mary daughters to Isaac Smith.
No. 20. 6 a. 128 r.

This lott belong to Ezer Sampson & Sarah Squin, grand children of Benjamin Squannamauy.
No. 19. 6 a. 128 r.

This lott belong to Saml Wood.
No. 12. 6 a. 128 r.

This lott belong to Sarah grandchild of John Sassmon.
No. 13. 6 a. 128 r.

This lott belong to Peter and Charles, grand children of Peter Wabuuk.
No. 14. 6 a. 128 r.

This lott belong to Richard Grandson of Sarah Dagett.
No. 15. 6 a. 128.

This lott belong to Deborah & Penelope, granddaughters of Peter Wabuuk.
No. 16. 6 a. 128 r.

This lott belong to Ellis Anthony & Sarah Titicutt.
No. 17. 6 a. 128 r.

This lott belong to Hannah Hall, daughter of John Yokine.
No. 18. 6 a. 128 r.

Daniel Ward dwelling house, lived 5 years in ye same about 3 acres improved & some of sd improvements made by Capt James Church, about 10 years ago.
This lot belong to the [House.]

Sarah Quam lived on this lot 9 years, improvement made one acre & three forths.
This lott belong to Sarah Quam & Hope Penny.
No. 10. 6 a. 128 r.

Abigail Titicutt lived on this lot about 25 years improvement made by Saml Titicutt about 1 [H.] acre. This lott belong to Nancy daughter of Francis Townsend.
(No. 9.) 6 a. 128 r.

This lott belong to Abigail Titicutt and Betty Cockaway.
No. 8. 128 a. 128 rd.

Thomas Amos lived in this house 3 years they say he bought of George Church.
This lott [H.] belong to George and Katty of James Church.
No. 7.—6 a. 128 r.

legall representative of Capt James Church.
No. 4. 47 acres 32 Rods.

This lott belong to the widdo of James Church, Jr.
No. 11 6 a. 128 rds.

Priscilla Ward lived (No. 2.) on this lott 9 years. [H.] 6. 128. Improv'r made three fourths of an acre.—Tom Pim no childn. This lott belong to Mercy Hope Isaac Church & Experience Ward.

This lott belong to Hannah Mouse & Elisth Penny grand children of Jona George.
No. 3. 6 a. 128 Rods.

Peter Quomey (No. 4.) lived on this lott about 6 [H.] 6.128. months improv't made about half an acre — Old Saml Church no post'y This lott belong to Deborah & Experience grandchildren of Lt Manchester.

James Wilcox, no posterity.
This lott belong to Joseph & Wm grand children of Lt. Manchester.
No. 5. 6 a. 128

Wm Page lived on this lott about 6 years improvement made Two Acres, who mark'd a grand daughter to Capt James [H.] Church. This lott belong to Eliath Nebe, grandchild to old Nebe.

22 rods 4 feet.

| 10 R 6½ | 10. 0½ | 10 - 7 ft. | 11 R. 13 ft | 12 r. 2 ft. |
|---|---|---|---|---|
| 3 acres | and 105 | rods in | | |
| | this angle. | | | |

91 Rods 6 ft for this Tear.

98 Rods 14 ft for this Tear.

98 Rods 14 ft for this Tear.

91 Rods 14 ft for ye head Tear.

This Plan was compuited December ye 5th 1763.

Watuppa

Pond.

# AWASHONKS

## THE SAKONNET - WAMPANOAG TRIBE

The old hunting grounds of the Sogkonates (Sakonnet) was in that territory now Little Compton, Rhode Island. The leader of the Sakonnet Indians was an Indian woman known as, Awashonks. History records her as, "The Squaw Sachem of the Sogkonates." She was an interesting woman, and a very good friend of Captain Benjamin Church, who owned and lived on a grant of land in her country.

The word, Awashonks, is believed to be an Indianized corruption picked up by the English, and recorded by its phonetic sound. We do know that the Indian word for queen is, Saunks. The guttural aspirate, "ewa" meant to the Indian either "The, it, that, a." The English may have continually referred to the Sakonnet leader as, "The Queen," to the extent where she and her people naturally accepted it by applying the Wampanoag word counterpart, "Ewa Saunks;" — and thus, Awashonks.

No matter; history records it as Awashonks, and Awashonks it is.

The squaw Sachem's husband was called, Tolony. Excepting his name, history records nothing about him. Awashonks and Tolony had one son who has been mentioned as a friendly Indian captain fighting under Church's command in the King Philip war. His name is recorded as Peter Awashonks, but his Indian name was Mamaneway. In a grant of land at the Wattupa Reservation, we noted with interest that the owners in 1763 were listed as grandchildren of Peter Washunks, (unquestionably, this same Peter Awashonks).

173

Awashonks also had several other children whose names were never mentioned. Among the leaders of her people who served under Captain Church in the war besides her son; — we note here, the Indian who was credited with killing King Philip. His name was John Alderman. Lightfoot was another of her people who served under Church as a friendly Indian captain.

The Squaw Sachem of the Sogkonates was first noticed by the English, when, on July 24, 1675, Peter Awashonks came to Plymouth with a group of Awashonks' people and signed an agreement of submission. A short time later, forty-two of her warriors made known their acknowledgment of their leader's capitulation.

An interesting detailed account of Benjamin Church's several meetings with Awashonks can be had by reading Mr. Church's own recordings of the events.

The contents of a letter from Awashonks addressed to Governor Prince, written no doubt by an interpreter, explained that she desired to send in all of her six guns, but that two of them were so large that her men were unable to carry them. We quote from the letter, "Since then an Indian named 'Broad-Faced-Will' stole one of them out of the wigwam in the night and is run away with it to Mount Hope . . . I shall not trouble you further, sirs, but deserving your Peace and Prosperity, on which I look at my own to be included, I remain your servant." It is pleasant to note that Governor Prince answered the letter after some delay, assuring her that the English welcomed her friendship.

We have noted, in the chapter on the war, Benjamin Church's meeting with her just prior to the breaking out of hostilities, and of the subsequent meeting during the war. For an excerpt of that meeting, we quote: "He pulled out his calabash and asked Awashonks whether she had lived so long at Wetusset as to forget to drink Occapeeches (strong drink). And drinking to her he perceived that she watched him very diligently, to see as he thought whether he swallowed any of the rum; He (Church) offered her the shell but she desired him to drink again first, he then told her that there was no poison in it, and pouring some into the palm of his hand supped it up and took the shell and drank to her again and drank a good swig which indeed was no more than he needed. Then they all standing up he said to Awashonks, You won't drink for fear there be poison in it, and then handed it to a little ill-looked fellow, who catched it readily enough, and as greedily would have swallowed the lot, when he had it at his mouth, but Mr. Church catch'd him by the throat and took it, asking him whether he was to swallow shell and all, and then handed it to Awashonks, she ventured to take a good hearty dram and passed it among her attendants. The shell being emptied, he pulled out his tobacco and having distributed it, they began to talk."

This meeting was held in Little Compton, Rhode Island, near the beach at the so-called "Treaty Rock" and the Squaw Sachem told Mr. Church that her people had only joined up with Philip because she did not hear from Church as was expected. She felt that, having not heard from him, the English had not accepted her word.

At about the time of this meeting between the Sakonnets and Benjamin Church, the Plymouth government was planning troop movements aimed at an attack on Awashonks and her people, but Church concluded the agreement in time to allow the expedition to be called off, with Awashonks agreeing to move her whole population to Sandwich, and to await further communication from Captain Church.

A few days later Benjamin Church met them at a point in Wareham, whose description tallies somewhat with the locality now known as Onset, Massachusetts; and it was here that Church recruited several of Awashonks' Indian warriors to serve the Colonists in the war.

The date of Awashonks' death is not known to us, but her grave is located within the old Indian burial grounds, half a mile distant from the Awashonks' Memorial Boulder in Wilbour's Park Woods at Little Compton, Rhode Island. This was one of the traditional spots pointed out to us by Mr. B. F. Wilbour, a sixth generation descendant of Benjamin Church's brother, Joseph. Mr. Wilbour also told us some interesting facts concerning other points of interest and events handed down to him.

## THE COHANNET - WAMPANOAG TRIBE

The Cohannet Tribe of the Wampanoag Indian Federation occupied the territory including parts of the present towns of Berkley, Mansfield, Norton, and Raynham, and also portions within the present city limits of Taunton, Massachusetts.

## SOWAMS; MONTAUP; KICKIMUIT; MUNPONSET

These were the royal seats of the various Wampanoag Sachems. We have mentioned Sowams as the favorite residence of Massasoit. The city of Warren, Rhode Island, is now on the site of this village.

We also have established the fact that his son, Wamsutta, (Alexander), preferred the tribal towns of Kickimuit and Munponsett. Kickimuit was located in that section of the country now near the towns of Swansea and Seekonk, Massachusetts. Munponset is now Halifax, Massachusetts.

Pometacom, (King Philip), established his residence at Montaup (Mount Hope) now located in Bristol, Rhode Island.

It has been said that these three villages were once the nucleus of the Wampanoag Federation, then known as the Pokanoket Tribe. The word Pokanoket later became the title extended to all the country occupied by the Wampanoag Indian Federation of the Algonquin Indian Nation.

## THE METTAPOISET and POCASSET - WAMPANOAG TRIBES

The wily and English-hating Corbitant was Sachem of the Wampanoag Tribute tribes known as the Mettapoisets and Pocassets. Corbitant was a powerful sagamore of the Federation. His domain spread into the area now occupied by Rehoboth, Attleboro, Fall River and Swansea in Massachusetts and included that section now Tiverton, Rhode

Island. He was believed to be the father of Weetammo. Corbitant's history figured so prominently
in many of our previous chapters that we find no
need for repetition here.


## THE CAPE COD - WAMPANOAG TRIBES

The WAWAYONTAT (Wiwiantic) tribe inhabited the area on the western boundaries of Wareham,
Massachusetts and close by the present Marion, Massachusetts.

The SIPPICANS lived within the confines of what
is now Mattapoisett and a portion of what is now
Marion, Massachusetts.

The KITTAUMUT TRIBE was situated within
the confines of the area between Plymouth and
Wareham, Massachusetts.

The COHASSETS hunted and lived within the
territory just above the present town of Marshfield,
Massachusetts.

The SAUGHTUCKET INDIAN VILLAGE was
located where now lies the city of Bridgewater,
Massachusetts.

The PAOMETS is another of the smaller Wampanoag tribute tribes that was located on Cape Cod,
Massachusetts. Their chief was known as Quaqua-
quaansuke.

The NOBSUOSSET was another small tribe located on the Cape. Their chief at one time was
called by name of Mashamiapaine. Other members
known to be in his tribe were, Little Robin Wah-
woonettshunke, Sabbatubkett and Sampson.

The COKASHOISE TRIBE was led by a chief known as Ashowoohanitt. Another lesser tribute tribe of the Wampanoags located on Cape Cod was called, the ASHIMUITT TRIBE. Akomont was their leader.

The SAKONESSET VILLAGE had a chief by the name of Pohunna.

The MANOMET TRIBE had a Wampanoag Sagamore as their chief. He was Cawnacome, one of the sagamores who affixed their signatures to the Treaty of Amity at Plymouth on September 13, 1621. Epanow, the Wampanoag sagamore from the Island of Martha's Vineyard, also signed his mark to this Treaty.

SHAWOMET was another small Wampanoag Indian village on Cape Cod. Their land extended from what is now Falmouth, Massachusetts to the west boundary of Mashpee, Massachusetts.


## THE MARSHPEE - WAMPANOAG TRIBE

The Marshpee Tribute tribe was first called, Massapee Tribe. It later was corrupted into the spelling, Mashpee Tribe; but the majority of writers preferred to spell it out as the Marshpee Tribe. After the King Philip war, the Marshpees absorbed the Coatuits, Satuits, Pawpoesits, Wakoquit, Ashimuit and the Weesquob tribes.

The Marshpee Tribe is famous by virtue of the survival of the "Old Indian Church," whose original edifice was constructed in the year 1684 and has remained a land mark on Cape Cod, Massachusetts, ever since.

It was at this church that the Marshpee Indians, following their conversion to Christianity, worshiped. Here, at this church, descendants of the Cape Cod Indian Tribes still assemble on certain occasions for tribal celebrations patterned after the gatherings known to the Wampanoags as the Nickommo and Miawene.

Within this area on Cape Cod, the last remnants of the local tribes found a retreat.

It is believed by some, that as late as the first few years of the 20th century, there were still to be found full-blooded Wampanoag Indians among the Marshpees. One source states that the last pure-blooded Marshpee Indian died in the year 1903.

We know that the Marshpees still claim to function as a tribe, and there are present inhabitants of the locality who claim to have considerable strains of Wampanoag Indian blood flowing within their veins. At the time of this publication (1957), Mr. Earl Mills of Falmouth, Massachusetts is their recognized Chief. Mrs. Winona (Coombs) Jonas and her family of New Bedford, Massachusetts, a member of the Marshpee Tribe, claims proof of kinship to the Wampanoag Sachems.

Many of these present Wampanoag descendants still maintain the customs and strong characteristics of their ancestors. A greater majority of them have intermarried with immigrants from the Cape Verde Islands, and have established themselves in large communities throughout the whole area of Cape Cod, Massachusetts.

From a clipping which appeared in the New Bedford Standard Times, dated November 26, 1935,

we quote, "The traditional 'Pipe of Peace,' which
the Indians once used to denote friendliness, was
smoked last night by the Indian Chief and white
settlers as a portion of the Indian Day program observed yesterday in that town, (Mashpee). This
ceremony took place in the Old Indian Church.
William James, known by the Indian name of Chief
High Eagle, Cyrus Edwards, and Ambrose Pells appeared in full Indian costumes."

In another article from the same New Bedford
newspaper, we find that during another Marshpee
Indian ceremony held in 1938, Mr. Ambrose Pells
was listed as their Chief "Rain-in-the-face."

Still another clipping, dated August 7, 1940, in-
forms us that Princess Red Feather of New Bedford,
Massachusetts, was one of the leading participants
at the annual ceremonies held at the Old Indian
Church in Mashpee. She sang three solos in her
native tongue as part of the rites in honor of Richard
Bourne, an early settler in Sandwich, Massachusetts,
who later worked and performed conversions among
the aborigines. Mr. Bourne was appointed a super-
intendent over the Marshpee Indian Reservation.

At these Indian rites held in 1940, delegations of
Marshpee Indians in their native dress, and others
from Mohawk Trading Posts in Concord, Fall River,
Lakeville, and New Bedford were present. Indian
leaders of this event were listed as Chief Black
Hawk of Pocasset Reservation in Fall River, Massachusetts; Princess Metasmqua, clear sky, who trans-
lated the appeal of the Great Spirit into English;
and Chief Hamilton and Natomaki (Sun Woman).

The location of the Old Indian Church and Burial
grounds is just northeast of the Mashpee traffic

circle on Route 28 on Cape Cod, Massachusetts.
From the names engraved on the old grave stones in
the cemetery there, one notices: Poknet, Chief Big
Elk, Princess Bald Eagle, Chief Deer, Little Chief
Haynes, Prince Blue Bear, Princess Yellow Bird, and
Chief Black Ox.

## THE CAPOWACK - WAMPANOAG TRIBES

From Cape Cod, Massachusetts, we sail over Buz-
zard's Bay to the Island of Nope, sometimes called
by early historians as, Capowack; but now called,
Martha's Vineyard. It is interesting to note that
Roger Williams called this same Island by the name
of Martin's Vineyard.

Here on this island lived additional tribute tribes
of the Wampanoag Indian Federation. They were
the tribes of the TAKEMMIES, THE NUNPAUGS,
THE AQUINNAHS, and THE CHAPPAQUID-
DICKS, collectively called, THE CAPOWACKS.

What was then Aquinnah is now known as Gay
Head. Takemmy is now called Tisbury, and Edgartown is now the location of an old Nunpaug Indian
village; and the Chappaquiddick village was in the
locality still called by the original name.

In Josselyn's account written about the Indians
of this Island, called "Account of Two Voyages into
New England," we are informed that the aborigines
of this section lived in several villages that were of
no permanency, "composed as they were of loosely
constructed wigwams, which their owners moved
about as they willed in accordance with the food
supply and the seasons." He also tells of having

seen, "a half hundred wigwams together on a piece
of ground, and upon having returned in a week or
two, he noticed that they were gone."

The main village of the Nunpaugs was situated
along the shores of the so-called "Great Herring
Pond." In later years Indians living near this pond
were called by the residents as, Herring Pond Indians. This pond is located in Maschachket.

The Takemmy Village was located near the Great
Tisbury Pond.

The Aquinnahs, later termed Gay Head Indians
inhabited that section of the Island now called Gay
Head.

The Chappaquiddick Village was in that section
off shore still called Chappaquiddick Island.

The Gay Head or Catachukutcho area, like the
Marshpee's, soon absorbed all the Indians of the
Island and to this day descendants of these tribes
live on the Island, and celebrate, in annual programs,
rites and customs handed down to them by their
ancestors. Like the Marshpees and all of the other
Wampanoags, their blood has mingled with that of
other races.

Legend has it that the gods of these Gay Head Indians were Moshup, the giant whose pipe ashes are
said to have formed Nantucket Island, and his wife
Squant.

These two gods contributed to numerous quaint
stories that may still be found in many accounts of
the tribe. Another of their gods was known as
Waukshos. Still another was called Washuanks;
another Wee-wank. In the beginning, Moshup was
solely the giant God of the Aquinnahs, and his resi-

dence was on that part of the Island now Gay Head;
but in our research we have seen his name springing
up in stories of other Wampanoag Tribes.

Of all the pure-bred Gay Head Indians, the Squaw
known as Tamson Week is best remembered. Leonard Vanderhoop was the last Indian to have tendered
service as watchman of the Gay Head Light. Deacon Jeffers is also recalled as an outstanding person
in Gay Head History.

Of the very early Indian Chiefs, the names of the
Indians, Mittark and his older brother, Ompohhan-
nut, appear as the sons of the Sachem Nohtoakfact.
Mittark and his brother both figured in a court decision in the division of lands at Martha's Vineyard.
Mittark later sold his share to the Earl of Limerick
in the year 1687. The Earl left it to a religious society, with the deeds ending up intestate.

Cheeschanmuck, son of an Island Chief, was an
Indian College graduate in the Harvard class of
1665, but he unfortunately died in 1666.

The better known Indian burial grounds are located near, or close by, the Gay Head Light, and at
Abel's Neck, and at Molitaiha's Hill.

Deacon Simmons was considered the last Indian
chief of the Gay Headers. Mr. Earl Mills, chief of
the Marshpees, recognized the late Rev. Leroy Perry
as the Great Sachem of the Wampanoags. Mr.
Lorenzo C. Jeffers is now successor to the sachemship.

One of the best known tales of the Gay Head Indians is the love story of Katamas, the ugly Indian
maid who fell in love with an eel, which later proved
to be a bewitched Indian Prince.

At the time of the first visit of the white man to the Vineyard it is said that the Indian population numbered into 3000 people. The aborigines of this Island were competent gardeners, taking care of large tracts of cultivated areas of tobacco, corn, beans and squash. The men of the tribes were excellent fishermen and employed wooden dugouts which seated from six to twenty men. These aboriginal craft were handled expertly; and they often ventured quite a way out into the rough waters surrounding their homeland. It is known that these Indians made frequent visits to the mainland by use of these small vessels.

The Island Indian's way of life and abode was in no great way different from the customs of their brethren on the mainland.

As we have mentioned previously, it is believed that the Norsemen may have visited the Islands in the year 1000; but, it is also founded on vague records that the navigator, Verrazzano, touched upon the shores of Nope in the year 1524.

In the year 1611, Captain Edward Harlow sailed from England, and it is known that he, too, landed upon the Island. During this expedition, two of the Indian natives were kidnapped and sold into slavery. One of these Indians was called, Epanow. In the year 1621, we find this name spelled Apanow (Epanow) on the Treaty of Amity signed at Plymouth, giving rise to the belief that this same aborigine was then the Sagamore of the tribes on Martha's Vineyard.

The story of Epanow is an interesting one.

## EPANOW

He was the Sachem of the Wampanoag Tribute Tribes on the Island of Martha's Vineyard and a sagamore of the Federation. We have already mentioned that he was kidnapped in the year 1611 by a white explorer by the name of Captain Edward Harlow. He was taken to England after his capture, and very cunningly told his captors of the vast amounts of gold and other wealth in his homeland. He managed to instill a great desire for this booty in their minds, and encouraged them to form an expedition in quest of these treasures with himself as guide.

Epanow's scheme worked; and it was not long afterward that he found himself on a ship headed for Martha's Vineyard. Upon arrival, Epanow managed to escape into the vastnesses of his homeland.

An old historian by the name of Gorges, in writing of another Englishman's visit to the Island said, "This savage was so cunning, that after he had questioned him (Capt. Dermer) about me and all he knew belonged unto me, conceived that he (Dermer) had come to betray him; and so conspired with some of his fellows to take the captain; thereupon they laid hands upon him, but he being a brave, stout gentleman, drew his sword and managed to free himself but not without fourteen wounds." This was written in respect to an attack upon a Captain Thomas Dermer who visited the Island and met up with Epanow who had bragged of his escape from the English.

## JAMES F. COOPER

The following is a reprint taken from the Vineyard Gazette, dated Tuesday, July 21, 1931:

"In previous articles carried in the Gazette, the statement has been made by elderly inhabitants of Gay Head that the Cooper family men are the only remaining residents of the Indian town who closely resemble the Indians of long ago. The appearance of these men has often been remarked upon by those who were impressed by their stature and features and it is no surprise in the light of what history has to say about the Indian to learn from the lips of Indian descendants themselves that these men are like those of the olden times.

"They are very large men, over six feet in height, splendidly proportioned, and with attractive features. They are highly intelligent and well informed and their complexions are scarcely darker than that of many of their Yankee neighbors.

"In their movements, the resemblance to the Indian of history may easily be noted. They do not appear to move rapidly, but somehow they accomplish a great deal without apparent exertion. Their walk is easy and their footfalls light. In their conversation, the Indian described by early missionaries is recalled. Their voices are low and musical and their speech refined.

"Mr. James F. Cooper is a native-born Gay Header, and has spent nearly all of his life there. His father was a full-blooded Indian, known and respected by all. The elder Cooper was a seaman, following the sea all his life. Whaling was the principal profession followed by the men of Gay Head. Therefore, when young James left home, he went directly to New Bedford, as many of his youthful friends had done, there to seek a berth aboard one of the square-riggers sailing from that port.

"In later years, Mr. Cooper figured as one of the heroic rescuers at the sinking of the 'City of Columbus.' For his deeds he received a silver medal from the Massachusetts Humane Society.

"He later returned to his fishing boat and gear, and for twenty-two years he fished off Nomansland, sailing out to the reefs and catching the cod which were salted and dried ashore. With this, the lobster-fishing in the Sound around Gay Head, and his farm, he has lived comfortably and happily.

"His farm is a large one, containing the 'real' Indian Hill, with its cairn and graves, and a part of the famous 'Witch Pond.' But beyond a mild interest, Mr. Cooper is concerned but little in the traditions of these places and visits them but seldom, although he is very willing to guide a visitor to the historical spots. He is the true type of the Praying Indian of history, who earned the trust and respect of his white neighbors by his whole-hearted embrace of the Christian religion and the customs of the white men."

## THE NANTUCKET TRIBE

About thirty miles south-southwest away from Martha's Vineyard, lies the Island of Nantucket, Massachusetts, where two more of the Wampanoag Tribute Tribes were once located. The Indian population on this Island at the time of the early settlers was said to be 1500. One village was located at the

West end of the Island and the other occupied the East end, Siasconsett and Medaket. The early chiefs of these tribes were Mannochamock, alias Wanackmamak; and the other chief was Nickanoose.

Mr. Abram Quary, who died about 1855, is believed to have been the last of the full blooded Nantucket Indians. He died of advanced age.

In the year 1665, Philip heard that an Indian who had mentioned his father's name disrespectfully, and who was, according to Indian tradition, a "traducer" to be avenged only by the loss of his life, was living at Nantucket.

King Philip, upon hearing of this, immediately departed for the Island with a small group of his men in search of the man, a Christian Indian known by the name of Assasamoogh.

This Indian was visiting a friend when a messenger rushed in and told him that Philip was on the Island looking for his life. So close did Philip come to catching Assasamoogh, that we have accounts of astonished settlers having witnessed Philip chasing the Indian through the fields of old Nantucket, finally losing him in the deep woods.

The white friends of this "praying" Indian stepped in and appeased Philip's temper with a ransom of nineteen shillings that satisfied the Wampanoag Sachem to the point where he agreed to return to Mount Hope without the scalp of the "Traducer."

*Mrs. Zerviah G. Mitchell, descendant of Massasoit in the ninth generation. Died 1895, at ninety years of age, at Betty's Neck, near Middleboro, Mass.*

*Miss Zerviah Gould Mitchell, age eighty years (1928).*
*Courtesy of Mrs. Clark, Lakeville, Mass.*

# Chapter XII

# THE LAST REMNANTS
# OF THE WAMPANOAGS

*This picture taken in May, 1957, shows Mrs. Winona Coombs
Jonas, who traces her descent from King Philip, and Earl Mills,
chief of the Marshpee Tribute Tribe of the Wampanoag Federation.*
*Courtesy New Bedford Standard-Times*

Having forgotten the "Nickommo" and "Miawene" rituals of their ancestors, descendants of the Wampanoags now have adopted the dress and romanticisms of the western aborigine, and attend so-called "pow-wows" as pictured above. This scene was taken in Middleboro, Massachusetts in 1954.

Courtesy Howard C. Mandell

# THE REMNANTS OF THE RACE

So it came to pass that, by the 18th century, the wigwam had all but disappeared from the Pokanoket country. The last remnants of the Wampanoags sought refuge in small consolidated groups and looked to the superintendence of the white man for a way of life that was suddenly forced upon them.

The quick step into a culture years beyond their own had left them little prepared to face it; but try they did. To some, the various Indian Reservations were welcomed havens. Others remained in the localities they knew best, staying close to the shores of the "bitter water bays," where the Englishmen's commercial and fishing ports sprang into a beehive of prosperity, and offered to their race the qualities of the roving and unsettled life of a seafaring occupation.

Thus, the Wampanoag Indian was drawn away from home, and in many cases became so involved in his pursuits that contacts with family and friends were lost forever.

In a report to the Massachusetts Senate in the year 1861, Mr. John Earle said, "It was found that in New Bedford, Massachusetts, alone, there were about one hundred and fifty persons of the Wampanoag Indian Race, drawn from various tribes, exclusive of the very considerable number at sea in New Bedford ships, whose residences were elsewhere. Only a few of them considered themselves permanently located in the New Bedford area, and seemed to be looking forward to the time, when they would return to the places of their nativity, 'finally to mingle their dust with that of their fathers.' "

Mr. Earle's report goes on to inform us, "The distinct bands, communities, or tribes, having funds or reservation, or which have had them and are recognized as wards of the State, are Chappaquiddick, The Christiantown, The Gay Head, The Marshpee, The Herring Pond, and The Troy of Fall River.

"The descendants of Indians, of whom there are considerable numbers in any one vicinity, whose descent can be distinctly traced, but who do not stand in the same relation to the State of Massachusetts are those of Dartmouth and Yarmouth. There are, in addition, considerable numbers, belonging originally to some of the tribes before named, as the Gay Head, Marshpee, etc., but who, having left them to reside elsewhere, have lost their original rights, as members of the tribes, and are not acknowledged as belonging to them; and some others, residing either in neighborhoods, or scattered abroad in the community, who originated from other sources, or whose descent is not precisely known, but, of whose identity as Indians, there is no doubt.

"Of all these," goes on the Senate Report, "it is safe to assume that there is not one person of unmixed Indian blood. There are a few who claim it, but their claim does not seem to have any satisfactory basis. When it is considered that the intermixture, both with the whites and the blacks, commenced more than two hundred years ago, and that, in the course of ten or twelve generations there has been an opportunity, from intermarriages among themselves, for the foreign blood early introduced to permeate the whole mass, and when it is considered, that the intermixture has been constantly kept up, from the outside, down to the present time (March 1851), it would be a marvel indeed, if any Indian of the pure native race remained."

Mr. Earle's report goes on to say, "Of the publishments of colored persons entered on the early records of Dartmouth, Massachusetts, by far the larger portion are those marriages of negro men to Indian women. In Yarmouth, a larger portion of those of Indian descent have intermarried with the whites, till their progeny has become white, their social relations are with those of that color, and they are mingled with the general community, having lost their identity as a distinct class . . . *and it would have been a fortunate thing for all the tribes, if it had been so with them all.* But the mixture in most of the tribes has been more with the negro race than with the whites, till that blood probably predominates, though there are still a considerable number, who have the prominent characteristics of the Indians — the lank, glossy, black hair, the high cheek bones, the bright, dark eye, and other features peculiar to the race.

"Much ignorance and misapprehension prevail in the community at large, among those who have not had the opportunity of personal observation relative to those remnants of their race. They seem to suppose that they have hardly emerged from their aboriginal state, and although the painted face may not now be seen, nor the war whoop, the tomahawk, nor the scalping knife be actually encountered among them, yet that they are not more than a step or two removed from these things; and the questions: "What sort of people are they?" "Do they dress like white folks?" "Do they live in Wigwams?" "Can they speak the English language?," or others of a like nature are continually asked. If the querist would reflect that, for more than two centuries, they have lived commingled in a community with the white race, or on their little plantations surrounded by them, and in constant intercourse with them, that they are few and the whites are many, and that the tendency of such bodies always is, for the few to assimilate to the many, especially where the latter have the stronger characteristics, they would hardly ask such questions as these.

"A large proportion of the males of the several tribes had always been sailors or laborers of various kinds, and were thus, almost from childhood, brought in constant personal contact and association with the whites, and so afforded them the opportunity of acquiring their habits, customs, and modes of thought. Many of the females, also, had been in service to various white families of elevated social position, where they became familiar with the manners and modes of civilized and refined living.

"These remaining people were nearly all poor, but some of them lived in homes that compared with those of others in the community of equal means. It was noted by many who visited these Indians, that their hospitality was always made with propriety, dignity, and good taste. It was always sincere, free of mawkish, or embarrassing apology, made or attempted, for the quality of the meals they extended to a visitor."

This same Mr. Earle, who presented the Senate report we have quoted here, had this to say; "It is granted that, like other people, they have those who are rude, vulgar, coarse, and degraded. But, in my visits to them, embracing nearly every family of all the tribes, and some of them two or three times, I have never met an incivility of word, look, or action, from old or young, and, though many of them are shiftless, improvident, and very poor, I have not seen, with but a few exceptions in two or three tribes, the squalor and extreme poverty and destitution that are often to be found among the lower class of whites in our large towns and cities.

*"It would be fortunate, if no shade more gloomy could be given to this picture. But the prejudice of caste, social exclusion, and civil disfranchisement, have done a fearful work with the race. (Indian). The weight which these have brought to bear on them seems to have almost crushed out even the wish to have it removed, and the mass appear to be sunk into that state of constrained apathy, with which we submit to physical evils that we know are inevitable. On them, moral purity, social refinement, and intellectual strength and culture, confer not distinction, or give them even an equal position to those of the dominant race who may be far their inferiors in these respects. Having never enjoyed equality of civil and social rights, the conviction seems stamped upon their minds, that, in being created Indians, they were necessarily doomed to their present condition, and that it is vain to contend against their destiny. Thus all aspiration is suppressed, and, where there is not aspiration, there can be no a-chievement. This feeling, however, is not universal. There are ardent spirits among them who are impatient of the guardianship, and chafe under the disabilities to which they are subjected, and who would gladly find some way of escape."*

We found that the whole expenditure of the State of Mass., for the benefit and support of the Indians, and for State paupers residing among the Indians, for ten years ending December 31, 1859, was $29,964.37. This amount included the sum of $2,500 expended for the construction and repair of meeting houses, school houses and other buildings for their use, but it did not include the interest of the Indian school fund, annually applied to the support of their schools.

## THE WAMPANOAG INDIAN CENSUS
### 1861

In the records of the Commonwealth of Massachusetts as of the latter part of the nineteenth century, we find the following census statistics of the various tribes remaining of the Wampanoag Federations:

## THE CHAPPAQUIDDICK TRIBE

At the time, the last of these people occupied the northerly portion of the Island of that same name, lying on the easterly side of Martha's Vineyard, from which it is separated by Mattakeeset Bay, forming Edgartown Harbor. The whole population of that tribe included seventy-four; with one family residing in New Bedford, Massachusetts, and one family in Edgartown, Massachusetts.

## THE CHRISTIAN TOWN INDIANS

These people found refuge in the little village of Christian Town, situated in the group of hills that skirt the shores of Vineyard Sound on the northerly side of Martha's Vineyard, and in the town of Tisbury. The group of inhabitants belonging to the tribe then was listed as fifty-three people, which included fourteen families.

## THE GAY HEAD TRIBE

The Western end of Martha's Vineyard is divided into three peninsulas, Nashaguitsa, Squibnocket, and Gay Head. They are nearly cut off from the mainland of the Island by Menemsha Pond which comes in from the north by a narrow strait, so shallow as to be easily fordable at low-water, and extends across to within a few rods of the south side, leaving an isthmus over which passes the highway to Nashaquitsa, and thence to Gay Head. Gay Head contains within its area about two thousand four hundred acres of land. In the year 1861, records show that about four hundred and fifty acres of the land were held in severalty, and were fenced and occupied by the several owners, and the remainder was held by the tribe in common. The whole population of this plantation, who at the time were recognized as having rights as members of the tribes, was listed as two hundred and four, which included 46 families.

(Direct descendants of the Indians still proudly maintain their residence to this day within the area once inhabited by their full-blooded ancestors of the Wampanoag Federation . . .)

## THE MARSHPEE TRIBE

In the year in which the source of this information was computed, it is interesting to note that this tribe's name had been corrupted into Mashpee. First it appeared in early records as Massapee . . . then

Mashpee . . . and to its present, Marshpee . . . In the year 1860 this tribe was located in the area of the District of Mashpee, and was considered the largest distinct body of the descendants of the Indians then remaining in the State of Massachusetts. It was situated on Cape Cod, Massachusetts, in the westerly part of Barnstable County, and is bounded on the north by Sandwich and Barnstable, on the east by Barnstable, on the west by Falmouth, and on the south by the waters of Vineyard Sound. The census of the tribe, at the time, was 403. This included 93 families. (Like the Gay Head people, there still are many residents of the locality who proudly point out their Indian ancestry, and still maintain annual celebrations and customs handed down to them.)

## THE HERRING POND INDIANS

This tribe had its habitation on the east side of Herring Pond, on a neck of land lying between that pond and Cape Cod Bay, the territory being chiefly in the south-easterly part of Plymouth; but a small portion of it was in the northerly part of Sandwich. The nearest point of access to it at the time was by railway station at North Sandwich, Massachusetts. The whole number of the tribe, excluding women who had married and lived with their husbands in other tribes, was listed at sixty-seven and included 19 families.

## THE FALL RIVER OR TROY TRIBE

The reservation of the Fall River, or Troy Tribe, was situated on the east shore of North Watuppa

Pond, in the easterly part of Fall River, Massachusetts about five miles from the business portion of
the city. The whole number so far as could be figured at the time of the census was seventy-eight,
and included 16 families.

## THE DARTMOUTH INDIANS

As we already have learned from the preceding
chapters, the Indians of Dartmouth country were
subdivided into the Acushnets, Acoaxets, and the
Apponagansetts, by which names some of the localities are still known to this day. At the time of this
census their descendants were still to be found in this
same region, comprised in the ancient town of Dartmouth, Massachusetts. This once embraced the present towns of Dartmouth and Westport, Mass., and
the city of New Bedford, Mass. The residences of
the Indians counted in this census were divided between these places, and the most numerous settlement of them was on the west side of the Westport
River. It was learned that a number of the families
emigrated to western New York, California, and
other distant regions, and still others, at the time of
taking this census, were said to be temporarily absent from the state. The number of those whose
residence was in this locality, or who were supposed
to have been only temporarily absent, was totaled
at one hundred and eleven, and consisted of 29
families.

## DEEP BOTTOM INDIANS

Some five or six miles westerly of Edgartown,
Mass., the road leading from that place to West Tis-

bury, Chilmark, and Gay Head, crosses a deep valley, which, commencing in the central portion of the
Island, slopes gradually southward to the sea. This
valley was called "Deep Bottom." Near its southern
extremity, a little way up the Western acclivity, was
a small settlement of Indians, called, from the name
of the valley, the Deep Bottom Indians. In the year
of the Massachusetts Indian census we find but thirteen people remained, and included but 4 families.


## THE MIDDLEBORO INDIANS

At the time of this census it was understood that
none of these Indians resided in Lakeville or Middleboro, Massachusetts. This tribe had been located in
the vicinity of what was then called Betty's Neck,
that section of land that lies between the Assawompsett and Long Ponds. The whole number claiming
to be Middleboro Indians at the time were listed as
ten, and included 4 families; 3 males and 7 females.
The 3 males were seafaring men; and two or three
families resided in New Bedford, Mass.

❋    ❋    ❋

As was destined; . . . the so called Indian Plantations and Reservations soon came to their inevitable
closing, and the Indians as a group no longer existed
in Massachusetts. For an example of legislation that
brought the closing of the no-longer needed areas,
we print portions of a bill presented by the City of
Fall River in the year 1907 in regard to an act relat-
ing to the Indian Reservation and Water Supply of
Fall River, Massachusetts.

"Section 1. Whereas certain lands situated in Fall River, in a section called Indian Town (Fall River or Troy Indians) lying on the easterly side of North Watuppa Pond, were conveyed to the province of the Massachusetts Bay to be held as an Indian plantation or reservation to the use and occupancy of Indians; and whereas the Commonwealth of Massachusetts has succeeded to the rights and title of the Province of Massachusetts Bay in said lands and may have obtained title to some part thereof by escheat or otherwise; and whereas there are apparently no Indians left on the same, except one family, claiming to be such, namely, that of Fanny L. Perry, occupying a small portion of the land of said reservation; and whereas as it is necessary that a part of said Indian reservation be owned and controlled by the city of Fall River for the protection of its water supply, now taken from said North Watuppa Pond; it is hereby enacted that the title of the Commonwealth to the parcel of said Indian reservation near said pond, and hereafter described be, and the same is, hereby conveyed to the said city of Fall River for the protection of the purity of its water supply; namely a certain . . . etc. . . ."

. . . and the act was so passed and went into effect.

So these too, met the fate of the other groups of Indians, descendants of the once Powerful Wampanoag Federation of the Algonquin Indian Nation.

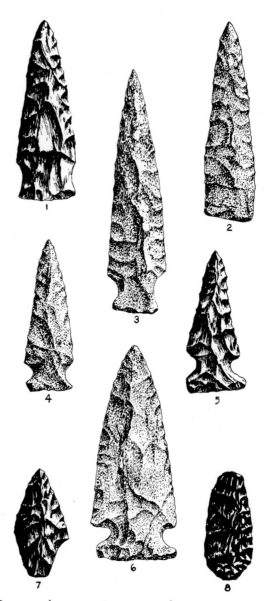

*Lance and spear points recovered at various sites in the Pokanoket country.*
*Courtesy Mass. Archaeological Society, Bronson Museum, Attleboro, Mass., Dr. William S. Fowler, Curator.*

# Chapter XIII

## ANAWON

### The Last Leader of the Wampanoags

### The Ultimate Collapse of a Culture

*Anawon, acknowledging complete defeat, humbly submits to Captain Church the royal symbols of the Wampanoag Federation.*

# ANAWON

In retrospect, we turn back the pages of time three centuries into tradition, and let the words and facts of the period recount the most dramatic and symbolic moments of the capitulation of one culture to another.

It was a spent and beaten old man in the person of Anawon, who humbly submitted to his captor, Captain Benjamin Church, the symbols and heritage of his Tribe, which had been handed down from leader to leader since time immemorial.

The only record found of Anawon previous to his connection with King Philip's war, is a notation of his appearance as a witness in 1672 to two sales of land by Philip to William Brenton and others. Aside from this mention, until the time of his capture, history recorded nothing of Anawon excepting mentioning that he was the Wampanoag Indian Federation's Chief Panseis, the Missinnege or leading Sagamore of all the tribute tribes.

We recall that as Philip ran in flight from Mount Hope, he was shot through the heart by the Sakonnet Indian ally, "Alderman." A few moments after this fatal shooting, Captain Church heard one of the enemy, who seemed to be a "great surly" fellow, shout in a loud voice, "Iootash! Iootash!"

Because this is the concluding event in the story of the final act of submission as a tribe, and the end of hostilities, we will quote from the personal story of the Victor. The following, we quote directly from Captain Church's own account: "Captain Church called to his Indian, Peter, son of Awashonks, and asked him, Who that was that called so. He answered, It was old Anawon. Philip's great Captain, calling on his soldiers to stand to it and fight stoutly."

Later, while at Plymouth, Captain Church received word that Anawon and about sixty of his followers were encamped in a section of the woods near Rehoboth called Squannakonk Swamp.

On September 9, 1676, (and again we quote from Captain Church's history); "There came a post to inform the Captain that early the same morning a canoe with several Indians in it passed from Prudence Island to Popasquash Neck. Captain Church thought if he could possibly surprise them, he might probably gain some intelligence of more game; therefore he made all possible speed after them. The ferry boat being out of the way, he made use of canoes. But by the time they had made two freights and had got over the Captain and about fifteen or sixteen of his Indians, the wind sprung up with such violence that the canoes could no more pass. The Captain, seeing it impossible for any more of his soldiers to come to him, he told his Indians if they were willing to go with him, he would go to Popasquash and see if they could catch some of the enemy Indians. So they marched through the thickets that they might not be discovered until they came unto the salt meadow (at Silver Creek where a gas works was later located) to the northward of Bristol Town, that now is. Then they heard a gun, the Captain looked about not knowing but it might be some of his own company in the rear; so halting till they all came up, he found 'twas none of his own company that fired. Now though he had but a few men, was minded to send some of them out on a scout. He moved it to Captain Lightfoot to go with three more on a scout; he said he was willing, provided the Captain's man

Nathanael (which was an Indian that they had lately taken), might be one of them, because he was well acquainted with the Neck (Mount Hope Neck), and coming lately from among them knew how to call them. (Nathanael, being recently captured, would know what the enemy's call or signal now was.)

"The Captain bid him choose his three companions and go; and if they came across any of the enemy not to kill them if they could possibly take them alive; that they might gain intelligence concerning Annawon. The Captain with the rest of this company moved but a little further toward Popasquash, before they heard another gun, which seemed to be the same way with the other, but further off; but they made no halt until they came unto the narrow of Popasquash Neck; where Captain Church left three men more to watch if any should come out of the Neck, and to inform the scout, when they returned, which way he had gone."

After spending a hungry and solitary night in the swamp, on Monday, September 11th, they resumed the business of seeking out Anawon and came upon Nathanael with ten captives, "two being some of his old acquaintances, he had great influence upon them, and with his enticing story (telling what a brave Captain he had, how bravely he lived since he had been with him, and how much they might better their condition by turning to him, etc.), persuaded and engaged them to be on the better side of the hedge. They all contended that it was very hard to find Annawon as he never camped in the same place."

At this time one of Church's Indian soldiers informed him that he believed his father was living in the woods about four miles from them and he re-

quested permission to go and get his father, which
was granted; but Church decided to go along with
him. "They heard the Indian soldier make a howl-
ing for his father; and later heard somebody answer
him, but while they were listening; they thought
they heard somebody coming towards them; presently saw an old man coming up with a gun on his
shoulder, and a young woman following of him in
the track which they lay by . . . He asked the young
woman what company they came from. She said
from Captain Annawon's." Further question proved
that they had been sent by Anawon to seek after a
group that had been sent to Mount Hope in search
of provisions.

"However, he (Church) asked his small company
that were with him, whether they would willingly
go with him and give Annawon a visit" . . . and
they agreed. The only Englishman with Church at
the time was one Cook of Plymouth, and he went
along also.

"Captain Church then asked the old fellow he had
just captured with the young squaw if he would pilot
him to Annawon. He answered that he having given
him his life, he was obliged to serve him. The old
man would out-travel them so far some times that
they were almost out of sight; looking over his
shoulder and seeing them behind he would halt. Just
as the sun was setting, the old man made a full stop
and  sat down, the full company coming up also sat
down,  being weary, Captain Church asked what
news. He answered that about that time in the even-
ing Captain Annawon sent out his scouts to see if the
coast was clear, and as soon as it began to grow dark
the scouts returned, and then said he, we may move
again securely.

"When it began to grow dark the old man stood up again, Captain Church asked him if he would take a gun and fight for him. He bowed very low, and prayed him not to impose such a thing upon him, as to fight against Captain Annawon his old friend. But says he, 'I will go along with you, and be helpful to you, and will lay hand on any man that shall offer to hurt you.'

"It being pretty dark, they moved close together through the woods and upon hearing the sound of corn being ground in mortars they learned they were close by Annawon's camp and soon came into view of it.

"He saw three companies of Indians at a little distance from each other; being easy to discover by the light of their fires. He saw also the great Annawon and his company, who had formed his camp or kenneling place by falling a tree under the side of the great cliffs of rocks, and setting a row of birch bushes up against it; where he himself, his son, and some of his chiefs had taken up their lodgings, and made great fires without them, and had their pots and kettles boiling, and spits roasting. Their arms also he discovered all set together, in a place fitted for the purpose, standing up on end against a stick lodged in two crotchets, and a mat placed over them, to keep them from the wet or dew. The Old Annawon's feet and his son's head were so near the arms, as almost to touch them.

"The rocks were so steep that it was impossible to get down, as they lowered themselves by the boughs, and the bushes that grew in the cracks of the rocks.

"Captain Church then ordered the old man and his daughter to go down foremost with their baskets at their backs, that when Annawon saw them with their baskets he should not mistrust the intrigue. Captain Church and his handful of soldiers crept down also, under the shadow of those two and their baskets. The Captain himself crept close behind the old man, with his hatchet in his hand and stepped over the young man's head to the arms. The young Annawon discovering of him, whipped his blanket over his head, and shrunk up in a heap. The old Captain Annawon started up on his breech, and cried out, 'Howoh.' And dispairing of escape, threw himself back again, and lay silent until Captain Church had secured all the arms, etc. And having secured the company, he sent his Indian soldiers to the other fires and companies, giving them instruction, what to do and say. Accordingly they went into the midst of them. When they discovered themselves, told them that their Captain Annawon was taken, and it would be best for them, quietly and peaceable to surrender themselves, which would procure good quarter for them; otherwise, if they should pretend to resist or make their escape; it would be in vain, and they could expect no other but that Captain Church, with his great army, who had now entrapped them; and keep every man in his place until it was day, they would assure them that their Captain Church, who had been so kind to themselves when they surrendered to him, should be as kind to them. Now they being old acquaintances, and many relations, did much the readier give heed to what they said; complied, and surrendered up their arms unto them, both their guns and hatchets, etc., and were forthwith carried to Captain Church.

"Things being so far settled, Captain Church asked Annawon, 'what he had for supper' For said he, I am come to sup with you.' 'Taubut' said Annawon, . . . and called the squaws to prepare a meal for the Captain and his men."

The two men supped together and afterward Church placed some of his men as guards about the camp. For safety sake, Church, lay himself next to Anawon's son in a position so that the young man's body was first exposed to danger should the captives decide a sudden means to escape. Anawon lay close by but it was quite apparent that both leaders could find no sleep. After awhile, Church noticed that Anawon rose and silently walked away. Expecting foul play, Church again gathered himself closer to Anawon's son but soon learned his anxiety was unfounded, for soon afterwards, Anawon returned and sat down by Church. He unrolled a bundle of deerskin and placed before the white man the symbols of office of his predecessor, King Philip. These treasured traditional pieces of the tribe included the broad sachem belt that told in designs of black and white wampum the histories and events of the tribes since time immemorial. Here was the "Holy Eucharist" or "Torah" of the Indians. It also included a smaller belt trimmed with moose hair with the design depicting the "Totem of the Wolf," the emblem of the Wampanoag Federation.

Laying these symbols of the once powerful Federation together with the two glazed powder horns and red blanket once belonging to Philip, the last Sachem of the Wampanoags, the great Indian Sagamore and leading Panseis of the Tribes, — now the defeated and tired old man, Anawon, said in good

English, "These you have now. *There is no Indian in all the land of Pokanoket worthy of its possession."*

Research has shown that these "Royalties" of the Wampanoag Federation were shipped in 1677 by Governor Josiah Winslow of Plymouth County to King Charles II of England.

Captain Benjamin Church, military leader of the Pilgrims, wrote, on September 10, 1676 that he had received from Anawon, "a bundle of deerskin containing the symbols of office of Annawon's predecessor, King Philip. Included were a broad wampum belt containing a pictorial history of the Wampanoag Tribe and a smaller trimmed with red hair (obtained from the Nipmuck Country) with a design depicting the 'Totem of the Wolf,' the emblem of the Federation, two glazed powder-horns, and a red blanket."

Records of the Massachusetts Historical Society, (Colonial Papers XLVI, Article 149) contain a copy of a letter dated "New Plymouth, 26th June, 1677" from Josiah Winslow, Governor, to King Charles II, in which the Governor "craves His Majesty's acceptance of these few Indian rarities, being the best of our spoils and the best of the ornaments and treasures of the Sachem Philip, the grand rebel; a belt of wampum nine inches (width) wrought with black and white wampum in figures and flowers, and pictures of many birds and beasts; (This, when hung upon Captain Church's shoulder, it reached the ankles) and another belt of wampum wrought after the manner of the former which Philip was wont to put upon his head (brow band,) two flags which hung down upon his back, and another small belt with a star upon the end of it which he hung upon his breast; all edged with red hair; the most of them taken from him by Captain Benjamin Church, (a person of great loyalty and most successful of our commanders,) when he (Philip) was slain by him (Church;) being his crowne, his gorget, and two belts of their own making, of their gold and silver." (This last phrase is interpreted to mean that the wampum beads used in the belts were the same material used by the Indians as money. We also know that it was an Indian ally named Alderman who actually fired the shot that killed Philip) . . . The facts above were all taken from the Massachusetts Historical Society Proc. 1863-4, Page 481.

After handing over these royal symbols of the Wampanoags, Anawon and Captain Church spent the remainder of the night conversing, with Anawon doing most of the talking, reminiscing about what mighty successes he had formerly in wars against many nations of Indians, when he served under Massasoit, the father of Alexander and Philip.

"Early the next morning, the Captain took old Annawon, and a half dozen of his Indian soldiers, and his own man, and went to Rhode Island; sending the rest of the Company to Plymouth." Later he returned to Plymouth with his prisoners and two days afterward went to Boston.

Church spent two days in Boston and upon his return to Plymouth, he found, much to his dismay, "the heads of Annawon, Tuspaquin, etc., cut off, which were the last of Philip's friends."

. . . There, in this last chapter, the reader has the story of the last official acts of submission performed by the Wampanoags as a tribe. Henceforth, they were no longer a Federation of people, with a purpose, or leaders.

Remnants of their tribes who did not submit to the colonists wandered as refugees to the north lands and to the west, and were absorbed into the tribes of their Algonquin brothers who later were persuaded to side with the French in devastating the occupied English villages to the North.

The white man's blood was left intact in the Pokanoket Country where it flourished and prospered, over the years, into the Nation of which it now is a part.

In retrospect, and all events assayed, and notwithstanding the inevitable; we can not but weigh the benevolence of Massasoit and his Wampanoag followers in the balance of what did happen; — and close by saying, . . . it was willed this way, and such are the facts.

Here, in this binding, is the greater part of all that is known of "The Totem of the Wolf."

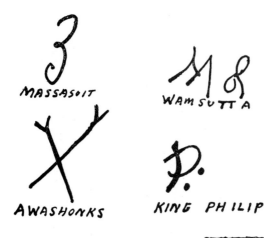

MASSASOIT

WAMSUTTA

AWASHONKS

KING PHILIP

THEIR MARKS

Copies of Four Original Deeds

of

Dartmouth, Warren, Bridgewater

and Attleborough

*To all People* to whom these presents shall come,
Osamequin and Wamsetto his eldest sone Sendeth
greeting

Know Yee that we the said Osamequin & Wamsetto
for and in consideration of thirty five pounds Sterling to
us the said Osamequin and Wamsetto in hand payd by
Thomas Prince Gent: Thomas Willett Gent: Miles Standish
Gent: Josiah Winslow Gent: for and in the behalfe of themselves and divers others of the Inhabitants of Plymouth
Jurisdiction whose names are hereafter specified with which
said summe we the said Osamequin and Wamsetto doo
acknowledge ourselves fully satisfyed contented and payed
Have freely and absolutely bargained and sold enfeoffed and
confirmed and by thes presents doo Bargaine Sell Enfeoffe
and Confirme from us the said Osamequin and Wamsetto,
and our and Every of our haiers unto Thomas Prince Thomas
Willett Miles Standish, Josiah Winslow Agents for themselves
and William Bradford Senr Gent: Thomas Clark John Winslow Thomas Cushman, William White John Adams and
Experience Mitchell to them and every of them, their and
every of their haiers and assigns forever All those severall
parcels and necks of upland Swamps and Meadows Lyeing
and being on the South syde of Sinkhunch Els Rehoboth
Bounds and is Bounded from a Little Brooke of water called
by the Indians Mosskituash Westerly, and so ranging by a
dead swamp Eastward and so by markt trees as Osamequin
and Wamsetto directed unto the great river with all the
meadow in and above ye sydes of both the branches of the
great river, with all the Creeks and Brookes that are in or
upon any of the said meadows as also all the marsh meadows
Lyeing and being wth out the Bounds before mentioned in

218

or about the neck called by the Indians Chachacust Also all
the meadows of any kind lyeing and being in or about Popasquash neck as also all the meadows lyeing from Kickomuet
on both side or any way joyning to it the bay on each side
To Have and to Hold all the aforesaid uplands swampe
marshes, Creeks and Rivers will all their appurtenances unto
the aforesaid Thomas Prince Thomas Willett Miles Standish
Josiah Winslow and the rest of the Partners aforesaid to them
and every of them, their and every of their haiers executors
and assignes forever And the said Osamequin and Wamsetto
his sone covenant promise and grant, that whensoever the
Indians shall remove from the neck that then and from thence-
forth the aforesaid Thomas Prince Thomas Willett Miles
Standish Josiah Winslow shall enter upon the same by the
same agreement as their Proper Right And interest to them
and their haiers forever.

To and for the true performance of all and every one of
the aforesaid severall Perticulars wee the said Osamequin
and Wamsetto Bind us and every of us our and every of our
haiers, Executors Administrators and assignes firmely by these
presents

In Witness whereof wee have hereunto sett our hands and
seales this twentieth day of March Anno Domini 1653

Signed sealed and

delivered in ye presence of us                    The mark 3 of

                                              Osamequin & a seale

John Browne

James Browne                              Wamsetto M & seale

Richard Garrett

## DEED OF DARTMOUTH

New Plymouth, November the 29th, 1652.

Know all men by these Presents that I Wesamequin and Wamsutta my son, have sold unto Mr. William Bradford, Captain Standish, Thomas Southworth, John Winslow, John Cooke, and their associates, the purchasers or old comers, all the tract, or tracts of land lying three miles eastward from a river called Cushenagg to a certain harbour called Acoaksett, to a flat rock on the westward side of the said harbour. And whereas the said harbour divideth itself into several branches, the westernmost arme to be the bound, and all the tract, or tracts of land from the said westernmost arme to the said river of Cushenagg, three miles eastward of the same, with all the profits and benefits within the said tract, with all the rivers, creeks, meadows, necks and islands that lye in or before the same, and from the sea upward to go so high that the English may not be annoyed by the hunting of the Indians in any sort of their cattle.

And I Wesamequin and Wamsutta, do promise to remove all the Indians within a year from the date hereof, that do live in the said tract. And we the said Wesamequin and Wamsutta have fully bargained and sold unto the aforesaid Mr. William Bradford, Captain Standish, Thomas Southworth, John Winslow, John Cooke, and the rest of their associates, the purchasers or old comers, to have and to hold for them and their heirs and assigns forever. And in consideration hereof, we the above mentioned are to pay to said Wesamequin and Wamsutta, as followeth: Thirty yards of cloth, eight moose skins, fifteen axes, fifteen hoes, fifteen pair of breeches, eight blankets, two kettles, one cloak, £ 2 in wampum, eight pair stockings, eight pair of shoes, one iron pot, and ten shillings in another comoditie. And in witness hereof we have inter-changably set our hands the day and year above written.

|  In presence of | } | JOHN WINSLOW |
| Jonathan Shaw | } | JOHN COOKE |
| Samuel Eddy | } | WAMSUTTA His mark |

## DEED OF ORIGINAL BRIDGEWATER

Witness these presents that I Ousamequin Sachem of the country of Poconocket have given, granted, enfeoffed, and sold unto Miles Standish, of Duxbury, Samuel Nash and Constant Southworth, of Duxbury, aforesaid, in behalf of all the townsmen of Duxbury, aforesaid, a tract of land usually called Satucket, extending in the length and breadth thereof as followeth, that is to say from the wear at Satucket, seven miles due east, and from the said wear, seven miles due west, and from the said wear, seven miles due north, and from the said wear, seven miles due south; the which tract the said Ousamequin hath given, granted, enfeoffed, and sold unto the said Miles Standish, Samuel Nash and Constant Southworth, in the behalf of all the townsmen of Duxbury, as aforesaid, with all the immunities, privileges and profits, whatsoever belonging to the said tract of land with all and singular, all woods, underwoods, lands, meadows, rivers, brooks, rivulets, &c., to have and to hold to the said Miles Standish, Samuel Nash and Constant Southworth, in behalf of all the townsmen of the town of Duxbury, to them and their heirs forever.

In witness where I, the said Ousamequin, have hereunto set my hand the 23d of March, 1649.

Wm. Otway (alias) Parker ⎱ Witness the ☞ OUSAMEQUIN.
John Bradford ⎰ mark of

In consideration of the aforesaid bargain and sale, we the said Miles Standish, Samuel Nash and Constant Southworth do bind ourselves to pay unto the said Ousamequin for and in consideration of the said tract of land as followeth:

7 Coats, a yard and a half in a coat    MILES STANDISH,
9 Hatchets
8 Hoes    SAMUEL NASH,
29 Knives
4 Moose Skins    CONSTANT SOUTHWORTH.
10 Yards and a half of Cotton

## DEED OF ATTLEBOROUGH

Know all men that I Wamsetta alias Alexander, chief Sachem of Pokanokett for divers good causes and valuable considerations me thereunto moving have bargained and sold unto Captain Thomas Willet of Wannamoisett, all those tracts of lands situated and being from the bounds of Rehoboth ranging upon Patuckett unto a place called Waweypounshag, the place where one Blackstone now sojourneth, and so ranging along to the said river unto a place called Messanegtaconeh, and from this upon a straight line crossing through the woods unto the uttermost bounds of the town of Rehoboth.

To have and to hold unto him the said Captain Willet and his associates their heirs and assigns forever; reserving only a compitent portion of land for some of the natives at Mishanegitaconett for to plant and sojourn upon as the said Wamsutta alias Alexander and the said Thomas Willet, Jointly together shall see meet; and the rest of all the land afore mentioned, with the woods, waters, meadows, and all emoluments whatsoever to remain unto the said Thomas Willet and his associates, their heirs and assigns forever.

Witness my hand and seal this eighth day of April in the year 1661.

Signed sealed and delivered

    in presence of

John Browne, Jr.                    The mark of A X A

Jonathan Bosworth              WAMSITTA alias ALEXANDER

John Sassaman, Interpreter.              his seal (L. S.)

# Bibliography

Allen, Zachariah. *Defense of the R. I. System of Treatment of the Indians* ........................... 1876

Apes, William. *A Son of the Forest* ............... 1831

Apes, William. *The Pretended Riot Explained* ....... 1835

Bicknell, Thomas W. *Sowams* ................... 1908

Bodge, George Madison. *Soldiers of King Philip's War* 1896

Bulletin of the Mass. Archaeological Society, Vol. VI, No. 1 ....................................... 1944

Bulletin of the Mass. Archaeological Society, Vol. III, No. 3 ....................................... 1942

Bulletin of the Mass. Archaeological Society, Vol. IV, No. 4 ....................................... 1943

Caverly, Robert B. *The Heroism of Hannah Duston and Indian Wars of New England* .................

Church, Benjamin. *The History of King Philip's War* Dexter ....................................... 1865

Denison, Rev. Frederic. *Westerly and Its Witnesses* ..

Dexter, Henry Martyn. *Mourt's Relations* .......... 1865

Diman, J. Lewis. *Annals of Bristol* .............. 1845

Drake, Samuel G. *The Book of the Indians* ........ 1845

Dubuque, Hugo A. *Fall River Indian Reservation* .... 1907

Du Pratz. *History of Louisiana* .................

Earl, John Milton. *Indians of the Commonwealth* .... 1861

Easton, Emily. *Roger Williams, Prophet and Pioneer* .. 1930

Ellis, Leonard Boles. *History of New Bedford and Its Vicinity* ....................................... 1890

Encyclopedia Britannica .......................

Freeman, Frederick. *History of Cape Cod Mass.* Vol. 1 & 2 .......................................

## 224 BIBLIOGRAPHY

Hare, Lloyd C. M. *Thomas Mayhew — Patriarch to the Indians* ....................................... 1932

Histories and Biographies of the First Settlers and older families as found in the Genealogy Room at the New Bedford Public Library, Mass. ....................

Hodge, Frederick W. *Handbook of the American Indian* .................................... Vol. II

Howland, Franklin. *History of the Town of Acushnet*

Jacobs, Sarah S. *Nonantum And Natick* ............ 1853

Joselyn, John. *Account of Two Voyages into New England* ...............................................

McKenzie. *History of the Fur Trade* ..............

Miller, William J. *Notes Concerning the Wampanoag Tribe of Indians* ............................ 1880

New Bedford Standard Times; & Vineyard Gazette, Martha's Vineyard, Mass. ....................

*New Standard Unabridged Dictionary* .............

Parley's, Peter Tales. *Lives of Celebrated American Indians* ............................................ 1843

Penn, William. *Works of William Penn*, Vol. II ...... 1682

Pierce, Ebenezer W. *Indian History and Genealogy* .. 1878

Ricketson, Daniel. *History of New Bedford* ......... 1858

Ricketson, Daniel. *New Bedford of the Past* ........ 1903

Rodman, Capt. Thomas R. *The King Philip War in Dartmouth* .................................... 1903

State Street Trust Co. *Other Indian Events of New England* ...................................... 1941

State Street Trust Co. *Some Indian Events of New England* ..................................... 1934

Sylvster, Herbert M. *Indian Wars of New England*, Vol. II ........................................ 1910

Tales of Cape Cod, Inc. (Bulletins) .............. 1957

*The Old Dartmouth Historical Sketches,* Vol. III ..... 1903

Tracy and Brothers. *Indian Narratives* ............. 1854

Trumbull, Henry. *History of the Discovery of America* 1830

Vanderhoop, Mary A. Clegget. *Gay Head Indians* ....

*Webster's Dictionary* .......................... 1944

Weeks, Alvin A. *Massasoit of the Wampanoags* ...... 1920

Williams, Roger. *A Key To The Language of America*
                                    1643—1936

Wood, William. *New England Prospect* ........... 1897

*World's Popular Encyclopedia* ................... 1937

# Acknowledgements

The task of collecting, comparing, and arranging the material for this book has been an absorbing hobby for many years. It has been a happy and fruitful undertaking, and richly rewarding to me in the many new friendships it has established.

The persons to whom I am indebted are so numerous that a complete listing of acknowledges is impossible. I am grateful, indeed, to all those who have assisted me in any way.

This work could never have been attempted without careful reading and study of the writings and records of the early explorers, of the original settlers of Plymouth, and of those later arrivals, who reported on their associations with the Wampanoags.

To Howard C. Mandell go my heartfelt thanks for his sincere and valued assistance in preparing the manuscript for publication.

I am grateful to Father Daniel F. Riley of Providence College for his kind words of encouragement.

The librarians in the various cities and towns throughout Massachusetts were valued helpers. Of these, Miss Marion H. Bonner, reference librarian at the New Bedford Free Public Library, deserves primary mention for her courtesy and assistance in helping me to locate much of the material within the voluminous collection of Town Histories on the Library's shelves. Miss Loretta Phaneuf, genealogical librarian in the same library, deserves similar acknowledgment.

For advice and confidence extended when it was appreciated, I gratefully thank Mr. and Mrs. Lawrence B. Romaine.

Mr. Everett S. Allen of the New Bedford Standard-Times also deserves mention for his interest and encouragement.

The old records of deeds and land titles were of exceptional value.

Finally, to all the descendants of the Wampanoag Indians, and to the Indians throughout the country whom I have interviewed within the years, I say; Be proud of your heritage! The contributions of your ancestors are indeed a poignant and patriotic chapter in the growth of our civilization. Massasoit, for his friendly assistance to the Pilgrims, should be accorded honorable mention among the company who earned for themselves the name of Founding Fathers of our Country.

. . . And, — to the person who was the object of my dedication, (whose wish to remain anonymous will be respected); Sincere thanks for your sympathetic inspiration. God bless you! May your prayers and hope for Indians throughout the continent be fulfilled!

MILTON A. TRAVERS.

# Index

*Notation. In regard to spelling:*
The author's research in this work has shown many complexities and corruptions in spelling: therefore, *this Index contains the most popular spellings.* (For one example and reason for need to establish popular spelling, see pages 15 and 16.

## A

T

*Excepting for those directly within quotes, dates used are
from the modern calendar.*

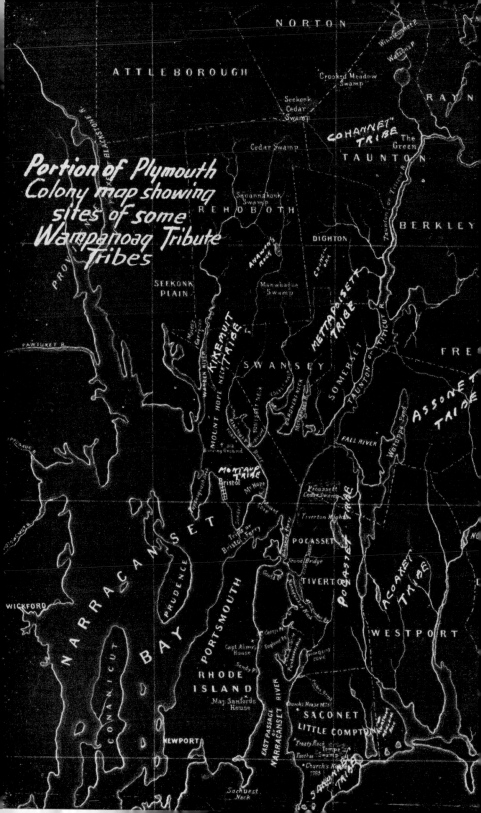

Portion of Plymouth Colony map showing sites of some Wampanoag Tribute Tribes